George Ernest Philip

Free St. Matthew's Church, Glasgow

A record of fifty-five years

George Ernest Philip

Free St. Matthew's Church, Glasgow
A record of fifty-five years

ISBN/EAN: 9783337283339

Printed in Europe, USA, Canada, Australia, Japan

Cover: Foto ©Lupo / pixelio.de

More available books at **www.hansebooks.com**

Free St. Matthew's Church, Glasgow

A Record of Fifty-five Years

By
George Ernest Philip
Session Clerk

✠

Glasgow
David Bryce & Son
1898

To

THE MINISTER,

OFFICE-BEARERS AND MEMBERS

OF FREE ST. MATTHEW'S CHURCH, GLASGOW

THIS RECORD OF ITS HISTORY

IS RESPECTFULLY

DEDICATED

Note

The following chapters are offered as a small contribution to local ecclesiastical history. By the many who either are, or have been connected with Free St. Matthew's, it is hoped they may be found of permanent interest and value.

The author is conscious that, while he speaks with full personal knowledge of more recent years, he has not a like advantage with regard to the earlier period. At the same time, with complete congregational records before him, and with the recollections of older members to fall back upon, he has not deemed it an impossible task to construct a narrative which, if less elaborate in details than might be permissible, should at least be accurate, and maintain a reasonable proportion throughout. He is hopeful that even a rapid survey of the past may tend to promote that *esprit de corps* which has so long been characteristic of St. Matthew's.

To the friends who have supplied photographs, or rendered other assistance, he desires to return grateful thanks.

6 Woodside Crescent,
Glasgow, 1st *November*, 1898.

Contents

Illustrations

I

Glasgow in 1843

"The year of recompenses for the controversy of Zion."

ISAIAH xxxiv. 8.

I

Glasgow in 1843

IT is not very easy for us, whose lot has been
cast in the closing years of the century,
to conjure up in imagination the Glasgow of
the early forties.

In attempting to do so, we must ever
remember that those were the days before an
aggressive architecture had broken down the
featureless lines of our monotonous streets,
and when the only public park we could boast
was *The Green*. If we except the hoary,
though as yet unembellished Cathedral, with
its western towers still standing, the venerable but dingy College in High Street, the
elegant Royal Exchange, some half dozen
well-placed churches, and a few quaint spires
and gables in the neighbourhood of the Tron-
gate, there were not many buildings in the

city which rose above mediocrity or laid any
claim to a distinctive character.

We have to think of a Glasgow entirely
divested of its stately warehouses and clubs;
of its spacious banks and insurance offices; of
its vast hotels and railway stations; of its board
schools and art galleries. George Square was
but a grass-grown enclosure, unadorned by
Merchants' House, General Post Office, or
Municipal Buildings, and Gilmorehill was
uncrowned by a palatial University. No
vision of a Christian Institute, a St. Andrew's
Hall, or a People's Palace had as yet dawned
upon merchant prince or city architect,
and the need of a Free Church College,
now so conspicuous from afar, had not, of
course, arisen. There was no network of
telephone wires overhead, there were no deep
shadows projected on the pavement by electric
lamps, there were no Cluthas on the river, and
no bicycles on the street. For Underground
Railways and District Subway we had half a
century to wait. Instead of ubiquitous halfpenny tramcars, the citizens had to content
themselves with an infrequent service of lum-
bering omnibuses, straw-bottomed and tartan-

painted, at twopence a head. Within a mile and a half of the Exchange a couple of toll-bars had to be reckoned with, and the *Herald* made its appearance but twice a week, in a single sheet, at the cost of fourpence-halfpenny. It is true that the noble river was ever in our midst, giving direction to the leading thoroughfares, and suggesting mighty possibilities to prophetic eyes, but the capacious docks of Kingston and Stobcross were non-existent, even ship-building yards were quite unobtrusive, and traditions of salmon fishing still lingered among frequenters of the Broomie-law and denizens of Windmillcroft.

The area covered by the city was insigni-ficant when compared with that occupied by the greater Glasgow of to-day. Eastward, westward, northward, southward, we have ever since extended, till ancient landmarks have become obliterated, and the cry is still for annexation. Perhaps the best way to form some accurate idea of the municipal limitations of those days is to examine for ourselves a reliable map of the period, such as is fortun-ately extant in that drawn by George Martin, surveyor, and dedicated to James Campbell,

Esquire, the Honourable the Lord Provost of
the City of Glasgow in 1842.   Let us then
unfurl the dusty roll, and take a rapid glance
at its bearings.

The South side, we find, was mainly represented by that oldest portion which still
rejoices in the mysterious designation of Gorbals, though Tradeston, Hutchesontown, and
Kingston, were just beginning to spring up
around it.   Crosshill, Govanhill, Kinning Park,
and Plantation were for the most part under
cultivation, and the sparse population responded to Sabbath bells by a weekly pilgrim-
age Clydewards, along the flowery banks of
a burn.   Pollokshields consisted of a few
isolated houses, visited occasionally by a
baker's van, but otherwise unacquainted with
the resources of civilization, and far beyond the
scope of police protection.   Even the specula-
tive builder was fain to confine his operations
within such reasonably extended boundaries
as Wellington Street, Cumberland Street,
and West Street.

Turning to the north side of the river we
find that St. George's Cross marked a very
extreme limit in a westerly direction, and,

in its vicinity, a recently erected church had just received the name of St. George's *in the Fields*. Beyond the Cross, New City Road and Great Western Road stretched right into the country, while Woodlands Road meandered pleasantly between hedgerows. It is pathetic to observe, faintly outlined on the map, ground-plans of attractive terraces, gardens, and carriage drives, which were never destined to be realized, and where now stand smoky foundries or ungainly tenements. Down by the river a dock is sketched, capable of accommodating so many ships of 300 tons each! Bath Street did not extend farther west than Pitt Street, which was then being opened up. From a sunny slope on the north side of Sauchiehall Street, a line of stately mansions looked out upon goodly orchards, the view being quite unobstructed beyond Douglas Street. The Crescents were in process of leisurely formation. Hillhead was as yet but an embryo suburb. Away to the north and west, the great residential estates of Kelvinside, Kelvinbank, Kelvingrove, Gilmorehill, Yorkhill, Overnewton, Burnbank, Sandyford, Woodside, Woodlands, and Claremont had not been broken in upon. St. Matthew's Parish Church, in the crook of lower North Street, occupied ecclesiastically the pioneer position westwards, and few buildings intervened between it and the rural village of Partick, which then rejoiced in its solitary constable, and the picturesque ruins of a castle.

According to the census of 1841, the population within the municipal boundaries stood at 255,650. To-day it is estimated at 705,000, or, if the closely contiguous suburbs be included, at 130,000 more. At the former date, thanks to the persuasive eloquence of Dr. Chalmers, seconded by the active beneficence of William Collins, William Campbell, and others, Glasgow was better off than she had ever previously been in the matter of church accommodation; yet the city and environs were then provided with but 75 Presbyterian places of worship as against the 240 of to-day. If, however, we are struck by the remarkable increase during the past half-century, another singular fact simultaneously arrests attention. Of the smaller number, it appears that two-thirds were connected with

the State, while of the larger, only one-third
remain in that relation. The moment we look
for an explanation, we are brought face to
face with the ever-memorable Disruption.

On the eighteenth day of May, 1843, as
every Scotsman knows, nearly five hundred
ministers voluntarily withdrew from the cherished associations of the Established Church,
throwing up status and emolument for conscience' sake. In this heart-stirring movement,
so little understood by the governing powers
of the day, the ministers were warmly backed
up by large sections of their congregations,
and in many cases where they hesitated to
lead, the people took action for themselves.
In Glasgow the tide of generous enthusiasm
for spiritual independence swept over the city
like a mighty flood, and within six months
no fewer than thirty new congregations had
been organized, twenty-three of these continuing to enjoy the ministrations of former
parish ministers.

As might be expected, a very serious difficulty at once arose in providing convenient
places of worship for so many homeless
flocks. While some of them, like St. Peter's,

St. Stephen's, St. Matthew's, and St. Mark's
were soon able even to improve on former
edifices and sites, others were compelled to
build where they could, and had long to
rest content with indifferent accommodation.
And so it came to pass that the Tron,
St. Andrew's, St. David's, and St. Paul's
got massed in line on the plateau of
Stirling Road, while St. Peter's, St. Enoch's,
Anderston, Hope Street, and Duke Street
clustered together in the hollow of Blyths-
wood Holm.

From this early and unavoidable dislocation
of parish boundaries, we seem to have got
somewhat easily reconciled to the present
anomalies of Free Church nomenclature.
Thus, the *Place* which once knew undivided
St. George's, has long ceased to be even
within call.   St. Enoch's flourishes on the
Kelvin, far from its *Square* root.   St. David's
has thrice withdrawn farther and farther from
the sound of the *Ramshorn*.   St. Andrew's
is no longer seen in association with the
Cross; and even the High Church has ex-
changed the murky banks of the Molendinar
for the clearer atmosphere of Dowanhill.

Duke Street Church is now in Mains Street, and Hope Street in Ewing Place; Anderston must be looked for in Hillhead, Hutchesontown in Govanhill, Stockwell in Pollokshields, and the Wynd in South Gorbals. Were anything needed to show the quality of the men, who in these modern days were called upon to suffer "for Christ, His crown, and covenant," it would suffice to recount the names of the "mighties" who presided over the congregations thus incidentally referred to, but we prefer to subjoin the entire list of those who, from the old Presbytery of Glasgow, cast in their lot with the Church of Scotland *Free*, adding by anticipation the University degrees by which they were latterly distinguished and best known. It is as follows :

Alexander N. Somerville, D.D., Anderston,   Died 1889.
Alexander Wilson, Bridgeton, -   -   Died 1891.
Robert Reid, Chalmers,   -   -   Died 1893.
John Cochrane, Cumbernauld, -   -   Died 1869.
Walter M'Gillivray, D.D., Hope Street,   Died 1880.
Alexander S. Patterson, D.D., Hutchesontown, Died 1885.
William Burns, D.D., Kilsyth, -   -   Died 1859.
John Lyon, Kilsyth,   -   -   -   Died 1889.
James Gibson, D.D., Kingston,   -   Died 1871.

Jonathan R. Anderson, Knox's,	-	Died 1859.
Thomas Duncan, Kirkintilloch, -	-	Died 1861.
Adam Forman, Kirkintilloch,	-	Died 1843.
James Macbeth, Laurieston,	-	Died ——
David Menzies, Martyrs',	-	Died 1877.
Robert M'N. Wilson, Maryhill, -	-	Died 1874.
Hugh Mackay, Milton, -	-	Died 1873.
Michael Willis, D.D., Renfield,	-	Died 1879.
James Munro, Rutherglen,	-	Died 1884.
Nathaniel Paterson, D.D., St. Andrew's,		Died 1871.
James Henderson, D.D., St. Enoch's, -		Died 1874.
John G. Lorimer, LL.D., St. David's, -		Died 1868.
John Smyth, D.D., St. George's,	-	Died 1860.
Thomas Brown, D.D., St. John's,	-	Died 1847.
John Forbes, D.D., St. Paul's, -		Died 1874.
William Arnot, St. Peter's,	-	Died 1875.
Andrew King, D.D., St. Stephen's,	-	Died 1874.
Joseph Somerville, St. Thomas's,		Died 1844.
John Thomson, Shettleston,	-	Died 1871.
Peter Currie, Stockwell,	-	Died 1859.
Robert Buchanan, D.D., Tron, -		Died 1875.
James M'Kinlay, Wellpark,	-	Died 1876.

Of these no fewer than six,—the Rev. Drs. Brown, Buchanan, Henderson, Paterson, Smyth, and Somerville,—were afterwards called to occupy the Moderator's chair in the General Assembly. To ourselves it is specially interesting that two,—Rev. Messrs. Anderson and Currie,—are represented in the Session of Free St. Matthew's by sons,

who have long been valued elders. Dr.
Gibson also, when appointed professor in the
Free Church College, attached himself to the
congregation.

As the eye travels down the column, what
gracious memories are recalled! How nobly
in after years did as many as were spared
to the city, stand shoulder to shoulder in the
van of every social, philanthropic, and religious movement for a whole generation!
Now all rest from their labours, and their
works follow them; but multitudes are alive
and remain, to whom the dignified presence,
the cultured conversation, the large-hearted
hospitality, the fatherly interest, the spiritual
solicitude of this or that one of the number
are amongst their most cherished and sacred
recollections.

We are sorry to miss from this honourable
roll the name of the minister of St. Matthew's
parish. The Rev. Peter M'Morland,—successor of Edward Irving in Regent Square,
London,—had been translated to Glasgow in
1839. He was a diligent pastor, and a good,
though not brilliant preacher. With sympathies
decidedly evangelical, he seems to have been

sorely perplexed as to the path of duty in
the difficult circumstances which so soon con-
fronted him.   When the crisis came, he did
not see his way to stand upon the Claim of
Right; but that some of his office-bearers
and people were of a different mind, the
succeeding chapter will show.

II
Founding of
Free St. Matthew's

" What shall one then answer the messengers of
the nation? That the Lord hath founded Zion."

ISAIAH xiv. 32.

Founding of
Free St. Matthew's

IT is no part of our present purpose to trace
the story of the "Ten Years' Conflict."
That has been told and retold in many a
glowing page, with which our readers are
doubtless familiar. It should be kept in mind,
however, that the ferment created by the
burning questions then agitating Scotland,
reached a climax in the spring of 1843, when
it became evident that decisive action was
imperative and imminent. A sense of un-
certainty as to the ultimate outcome of events
took possession of men's minds. It was seen
that some of those who had talked most
loudly against the reckless encroachments of
the civil power, were wavering as to the

B

attitude they should assume. Others had all
along judged it prudent not to commit themselves. But it was even more abundantly
evident that many who had hitherto been
serious observers only, were silently preparing
to quit themselves like men.

The feeling prevalent in old St. Matthew's
has been faithfully preserved in an interesting
narrative, by four elders, prefixed to the first
session minute-book of Free St. Matthew's.
"In the month of April," they say, "we
became more and more disturbed on considering our position in reference to the
proceedings of the evangelical party in the
church. Mr. M'Morland, our minister, had
kept back from any decided declaration of his
views in regard to the approaching disruption,
and it seemed more certain every day that
he would adhere to the moderate party, at
least to that party which was prepared to
accept the emoluments offered by the State,
on the footing that it will submit to compul-
sion by the patrons and civil tribunals in the
ordination of ministers and the performance
of their spiritual acts."

The admirable men whom Providence

brought to the front, in the delicate situation thus created, were :

1. Mr. Allan Buchanan, of George Buchanan & Sons, calenderers, Candleriggs, residing in Woodside Place, and uncle of the present Dr. George Buchanan, the distinguished Professor of Surgery in Glasgow University. He had joined the congregation a few years before from St. John's, where his brother remained a leading office-bearer, and was admitted an elder in 1840.

2. Mr. David Stow, of Stow, Wilson & Co., merchants and manufacturers, Buchanan Street, residing in one of the large detached houses on the north side of Sauchiehall Street. He had long been a prominent educationist in the city, and a trusted adviser of the Government in such matters. His name had become specially identified with the system of infant schools, and with the Normal Seminary, the first of its kind in Great Britain, which he founded. He was also the author of several publications on his favourite themes, one of which, a pretty bulky volume, ran through eleven editions. He had been one of Dr. Chalmers's original elders in St. John's,

and continued to correspond with him on the subject of Sabbath schools, after the Doctor's removal to St. Andrews. He was admitted an elder of St. Matthew's in 1842.

3. Mr. James Keyden, of Strang, Yuille & Keyden, writers, St. George's Place, residing in Newton Place. He was at the head of a firm, still honourably known in the profession, and was ordained an elder in 1840.

4. Mr. Peter Lawson, afterwards of Dron & Lawson, engineers, Anderston, residing in North Street. He was a plain hard working man, but a grand specimen of the good Scottish elder, and on him, in after days, Dr. Miller peculiarly relied. He was ordained in 1841.

The first was pre-eminently a man of action, the second a man of ideas, the third a man of business, and the fourth, a man of sense. They formed a unique quartette, in many respects the complements of each other, and were the four corner-stones on which Free St. Matthew's at first rested; the living foundation on which it was reared. After several meetings for prayer among themselves, they requested Mr. M'Morland to convene a meeting of Session, which he apparently pro-

ALLAN BUCHANAN.

DAVID STOW.

WILLIAM CUMMING.
Session Clerk, 1846-1876.

JAMES KEYDEN.

PETER LAWSON.

mised, but omitted to do. They thereupon drew up, and published in the *Scottish Guardian* the following resolutions :

1. "That it is now fixed and settled as part of the civil law of this country, that ministers continuing in connection with the Church of Scotland are bound under civil penalties to receive and admit all qualified persons who are presented to parishes by the patrons of these parishes, notwithstanding the unanimous and most determined opposition of the people, and although actual force should be required to enable them to complete the act of ordination.

2. "That it has also been fixed and settled as part of our civil law, that the civil courts are supreme in ecclesiastical matters, so that the qualifications of ministers come in the end to be determined by them alone, and, by means of these two principles of law, patrons are enabled to force in the most unacceptable presentees, and do utter violence to the feelings of the people, and to the consciences of the presbyteries, who are forced to perform these acts of ordination.

3. "That no grosser cases than those of Auchterarder and Marnoch,—in both of which the people were all but unanimously opposed to the presentees, and in one of which the majority of the Presbytery was also conscientiously opposed to the settlement,—can again occur ; and that the ministers and office-bearers who shall remain in the church upon the positive footing and condition that they approve of forcing in their ministers, and ratify the act of doing so, thereby come under an absolute obligation to commit similar acts when required upon every future occasion.

4. "That although various statements have been made

as to propositions for a modified liberty to the Church
of Scotland, all those propositions are based upon an
absolute acquiescence by the church in the above-men-
tioned settlements, and consequently in the principles
upon which they are founded, and that this Session,—
at least those members of it who subscribe these resolutions,—feel themselves constrained, by a sense of duty,
to declare that they do not believe that such settlements
and principles are reconcilable with the Word of God,
and the mind and will of Christ, the sole King and
Head of His Church, in matters spiritual, or that it
is, or can be reconciled with their duty to Him, that
they should, by continuing in connection with an Established Church based upon such principles, sanction and
consent to them," etc., etc.

This manifesto had no sooner appeared in
print, than Mr. M'Morland hastened to
summon the desired meeting of Session. The
four elders duly attended, handed in their
resolutions, and, having seen that they were
properly recorded, retired. Their next step
was to call a meeting of those members of
St. Matthew's who sympathized with their
views. This was held in St. Peter's Church,
and was addressed by the Rev. Dr. Robert
Buchanan and the Rev. William Arnot. At
the close, 200 persons gave in their names
as adhering to the principles of non-intrusion
and spiritual independence.

On the 6th day of May, the first of a series of meetings for prayer and business was held in a school-room in Bothwell Street. They were sometimes presided over by a neighbouring minister, sometimes by one of the elders, and they seem to have been a source of enjoyment and profit. It is also recorded, with gratitude to God, that "in addition to these, we were enabled to meet together for more private fellowship as a Session, to which we mainly ascribe it, that we have been blessed with a spirit of amity and love among ourselves."

Though comparatively small in numbers, the little band never seems to have doubted that it would one day be formed into a congregation, and it is expressly noted that those who composed it felt bound by old associations to remain in St. Matthew's district. One of their earliest acts was to divide the parish into sections, for each of which collectors were appointed, Mr. Buchanan being treasurer.

Matters progressed pretty rapidly, for under date 24th May, 1843, while the historic Assembly was still in session, we find it stated that, considerable subscriptions having been obtained, a committee was appointed to look out for a suitable site, which, after much deliberation, was ultimately fixed upon, in Kent Road, opposite the present St. Andrew's Halls. On the 11th October, the foundation stone of a church was laid by Mr. Buchanan, senior elder; and the Rev. Messrs. Arnot, Scott, and Somerville are mentioned as having been present. The weather was unfortunately so inclement that no address could be delivered to the assembled people.

Building operations were continued through the winter, the small congregation being meantime most kindly accommodated by the minister and people of Free St. Peter's. By April of the following year the first Free St. Matthew's was completed, and the sub-joined account of the opening is taken from the *Scottish Guardian* :

"This church, which has been erected off North Street, near Elmbank Crescent, was opened for public worship on Sabbath, 14th April. The Rev. Mr. Arnot of St. Peter's preached in the forenoon, the Rev. Mr. Brown of St. James's in the afternoon, and the Rev. Mr. Somerville of Anderston in the evening. The church is built in the Gothic style, combining simplicity and neatness with economy and comfort. The cost of the building is about £1200, and the number of sittings a little under 900. The church is surmounted with a small spire, furnished with a bell, the first that has been rung in Glasgow belonging to the Free Church. The church is a great ornament to the neighbourhood, in which it was very much wanted, being about half a mile from any other Free Church."

This may be recognized by some as the Free West Church of to-day. At the close of the first financial year, in March, 1844, Mr. Buchanan, the treasurer, was able to announce that £163 4s. 7d. had been remitted to Edinburgh for the Sustentation Fund, and that £600 18s. 4d. had been received towards the Building Fund.

All this was encouraging in a high degree, but as yet little progress had been made towards securing the services of a suitable pastor. Not that the good elders had been inert in the matter; far from it. "We turned our eyes," they write, "in various directions; but for a long time in vain. At one period we had great hopes that the Rev. Mr. Welsh of Liverpool might have accepted our call, and he was much inclined to do so, but Providence threw difficulties in our way, and we were restrained from what we desired. His discourse on the sufferings and atonement of Christ made a very deep impression on the congregation, and there was but one mind as to his being a man of God and a valuable pastor. We opened communication with various other ministers with the view of calling, such as Mr. Chalmers of Dailly, Mr. Agnew, and others, but from one cause and another we did not succeed in getting those whom we would have called, and in other cases the people did not proceed to call the ministers we had in view."

In the course of this anxious time Dr. Candlish had thrown out the suggestion that perhaps Mr. Samuel Miller of Monifieth might prove available. No time was lost in following up this clue, but not the slightest encouragement was met with, and the quest had to be abandoned.

It was not very long, however, before two circumstances occurred which unexpectedly changed the aspect of affairs. A rumour got abroad that Mr. Miller was on the point of receiving another call from a Manchester congregation, and also that the biting spring

winds of the East Coast were so affecting
him, that the doctor had actually urged a
permanent escape from their severity. Negotiations were immediately reopened, and Mr.
Miller's reply was this time to the effect that,
while personally he had no wish whatever to
leave Monifieth, yet, as the doctor had ad-
vised a change, and as two calls were now
before him, he intended to leave the whole
matter in the hands of his Presbytery.
Though it does not appear that the people
of St. Matthew's were particularly sanguine
of success, they appointed commissioners to
prosecute their interests before that court.

The following brief account of the proceedings is from the *Witness* of 9th October, 1844.

"The Free Church Presbytery of Dundee met at Monifieth on the 3rd instant, to take up the competing calls
to the Rev. Samuel Miller from Manchester and Free St.
Matthew's Church, Glasgow. There appeared at the bar
of the Presbytery the Rev. William Wilson of Carmylie
and Mr. Galt of Manchester; and the Rev. James Gibson,
Mr. Allan Buchanan, and Mr. James Keyden from the
Session, with Messrs. Wingate and Mirrlees, jun., from the
congregation of St. Matthew's. Parties were fully heard
and removed, when it was moved by Rev. James Miller
of Monikie (father of our future minister), seconded by Rev.
D. B. Mellis of Tealing, that Mr. Miller be translated to

the charge of the congregation of Free St. Matthew's, Glasgow. The motion was agreed to without a vote. We understand that Mr. Miller is to dispense the sacrament to the congregation of Free St. Matthew's at the approaching communion."

On the 25th of October, 1844, Mr. Miller was duly inducted to his new pastoral charge by the Presbytery of Glasgow, the Rev. Mr. Findlay of Camlachie presiding, and on the next day he was introduced to his people by the Rev. John Roxburgh, of Dundee, who was himself shortly afterwards to be transferred to this city. On the following Sabbath, Mr. Miller was assisted at the communion by his father, preaching his own first sermon as minister of St. Matthew's from the words: "O my dove, that art in the clefts of the rock, in the secret places of the stairs, let me see thy countenance, let me hear thy voice; for sweet is thy voice, and thy countenance is comely." And thus, to quote the concluding words of the narrative already referred to, "by the good providence of God, our prayers were answered, and a stated pastor, acceptable to the congregation, was settled among us."

III

Early Years of Dr. Miller's Ministry.   1844-50

"How beautiful upon the mountains are the feet of him that bringeth good tidings, that publisheth peace; . . . that saith unto Zion, Thy God reigneth."

ISAIAH lii. 7.

Early Years of Dr. Miller's Ministry. 1844-50

MR. MILLER, who, at the time of his coming to Glasgow, had reached his thirty-fourth year, was, as we have seen, a son of the manse. His early education had been acquired under the paternal roof, in company with three or four gentlemen's sons, who boarded in the family, and shared with him the advantage of a private tutor. When barely fourteen he was considered fit for St. Andrews University, which he accordingly entered, in the same year that Dr. Chalmers joined its professoriate. Young Miller had been commended to the kindly interest of this king among men, and it is not difficult to believe that the results of such an introduction proved deep and lasting.

In recalling those days long afterwards, Dr. Miller himself takes us behind the scenes. " During my second winter," he says, " four of us met regularly in Dr. Chalmers' house on Sabbath evenings, when he instructed us and dealt with our souls as if we had been his own children." Of a subsequent session, when one and another had gained admission to this family gathering, until the professor's large dining-room was crammed with students, he continues : " His instructions now became a kind of prelection to silent auditors on the leading topics of Christian doctrine and personal religion. Very simple and conversational they were, but all the more valuable on that account. We felt that we learned more of really Christian ethics at these meetings than from all his class-room lectures on Moral Philosophy."

Having passed through the usual college curriculum, Mr. Miller was licensed as a preacher in 1832, and in September, 1835, was ordained to the small parish of Monifieth in Forfarshire, not far distant from his father's manse. In 1840 he married Thomasina, daughter of the Rev. Dr. Ireland of North Leith, a gentleman who used jocularly to describe himself as "the oldest colleague in the Church," he having served in that capacity for twenty-four and a half years as junior to Rev. Dr. Johnstone. Mrs. Miller at once proved a valuable helpmeet in her husband's rural labours, giving earnest of the powerful influence she was soon to exercise in all the missionary and benevolent enterprises of a great city congregation. Amid these happy surroundings the future minister of St. Matthew's carried on his work, beloved by the whole country-side, and adding daily to his own equipment, till the circumstances arose which led to his removal to Glasgow in 1844.

From the pen of Dr. Thomas Smith we have a sketch of Mr. Miller, which even those who can only recall his later appearance in the pulpit, will regard as true to life. "From the first," he says, "it was manifest that his ministry was to be of no ordinary kind. With a splendid physique, and a graceful because unaffected delivery, with a

c

mind originally strong and admirably culti-
vated, with a heart overflowing with love to
God and love to man, and not inexperienced
in the workings of the Gospel and the Spirit
of God upon the affections, emotions, and
will, he went among his people in the fulness
of the blessing of the gospel of Christ. He
had a dignity that made his kindliness more
attractive, and a kindliness that rendered his
dignity all the more imposing. Apart from
his kindliness, his dignity might have been
taken for pride. Apart from his dignity, his
kindness might have been regarded as mere
good-nature. So admirably were the two
qualities combined in him, that no one was
likely to fall into either mistake, or if any
one did, it was sure to be rectified on a little
closer acquaintance. Deeply impressed with
a sense of the importance of his office, and
of the weight of his responsibility, his preparation for the pulpit was most laborious.
But it was a labour of love. At first his
sermons were carefully composed and fully
written. Latterly he was one of the best
of extemporaneous preachers."

Mr. Miller had no sooner settled in his

Yrs. faithfully
Samuel Miller.

new sphere, than he set himself with courage
and assiduity to the great task of building up
a powerful congregation in the west end of
Glasgow, which might speedily be able to
help others. The Kirk-session was convened
for the week following his induction, and
the following interesting extract is from its
minute, of date 30th October, 1844 :

"At this the first recorded meeting of Free St. Matthew's
Session, the members of the court are—the Rev. Samuel
Miller, minister, with Messrs. David Stow, Allan Buchanan,
James Keyden, and Peter Lawson, elders. These elders
have already constituted a Kirk-session (though no minutes
have been kept), under the moderatorship of the Rev.
Wm. Arnot of St. Peter's, by appointment of the Presbytery. There have been no deacons in the congregation
up to this date. Mr. Keyden is now unanimously appointed
Session-clerk, and has entered upon the duties of the
office."

Able as were the men here enumerated, it
is obvious that they could not long continue
to discharge alone the whole of the duties
devolving on the office-bearers of a growing
congregation. One of their earliest acts therefore was to call for an addition to their
number, as well as for such a staff of
deacons as would be able to cope with the
financial details incident to a church consti-

tuted like our own. By the end of the year all these arrangements had been completed, and attention could be freely directed to the needs of the poorer district adjacent to the church.

Mission and Sabbath School work have ever been conspicuous features in the life of St. Matthew's, and it is specially interesting to note their first beginnings. As early as May, 1845, we find a movement among the ladies of the congregation to set on foot a " School of Industry " in Anderston, no fewer than fourteen backing up pecuniary aid by the still more valuable offer of personal help as visitors. A female teacher was appointed at a salary of £25 per annum, with free house, the Deacons' Court granting use of the school-room behind the church till other accommodation could be found.

In the autumn of 1846 a farther step was taken by the opening of a day school in rented premises, under the charge of Mr. Robertson, teacher, and seventy children were very soon reported as in attendance. A Sabbath school was added in the following year. It met in the same place, and was superintended by volunteer teachers from the congregation, who formed themselves into the original "Sabbath School Society," which has since had such a long and honourable career under the wise rules which the Session then drew up for its guidance.

The great need for ordinary education was keenly felt by Christian men in those days, when as yet the nation had not awaked to its responsibility in the matter, and the eager use made of such opportunities as were provided soon led to the adoption of more thorough-going measures than had at first been contemplated. Along with Mr. David Stow other members of Session strongly sympathized with this benevolent enterprise. Mr. Allan Buchanan in particular never rested till a site had been secured, on the north side of Main Street, Anderston, for permanent mission premises. He collected subscriptions sufficient, with a Government grant, to permit the erection of what soon became known as "Free St. Matthew's School." This building long continued to be the centre of aggressive operations for the spiritual and temporal good of the district, and the mention of it even

now recalls hallowed associations to many.
On the last Sabbath of 1847 it was opened
as a preaching station by Mr. Miller, and
on the Monday following as a day school,
on which occasion the Revs. Dr. James Henderson and William Arnot attended as a
deputation of Presbytery, and addressed the
children.

For about a year prior to this, Sabbath
services had been held in the temporary
school-room for the benefit of the non-church-
going. They had been started by four
students attending the Free Church College,
but these gentlemen were unable to continue
their help beyond the month of April. So
encouraging, however, had this branch of the
work become that the Session felt it could
not be given up, and accordingly appointed
the moderator and Mr. Buchanan a committee to look out for a suitable agent to
carry it on for the future. It was not long
before they were in a position to recommend
for the post Mr. Allan M'Vean, a man with
whose spirit and qualifications they were well
satisfied. It was at the same time intimated
that the Deacons' Court had resolved to pro-

vide a salary of £15 per half year for a
catechist or missionary. The Kirk-session
"thereupon resolved to appoint Mr. M'Vean
to this work, and he is hereby so appointed
accordingly, it being left to the moderator to
give him instructions as to his duties, and
generally to superintend the performance of
them."

This was the first of a long series of
appointments which have followed, but to
which individually we shall not be able to
refer. The missionary assistants so chosen
were sometimes students or laymen, but more
generally probationers, and they discharged
varying functions, according as the work laid
upon them was confined to the mission district, or included a share of congregational
duty. It will be seen from the lists, which
we give at the end, how many of these
subsequently filled important spheres; nor can
it be doubted that the training received in
St. Matthew's both recommended and fitted
them for the greater life-work to which they
were called.

While Christian activities were multiplying
at the mission, it must not be supposed

that the increasing body of young people connected with the church itself were overlooked. In 1848, we find the Session anxiously considering the propriety of opening a Sabbath school for their benefit ; and a committee was appointed to make arrangements. Early in the following year, Mr. Nielson was able to report that a commencement had already been made with an attendance of twenty-five. The hour of meeting was 9.30 a.m. In these various ways substantial beginnings of strenuous work were effected—an earnest of wonderful developments yet to follow both at church and mission.

A reference to the Communion Roll of this period not only shows the large numbers who from the first flocked to Mr. Miller's ministry, but reveals the curious variety of elements which went to form the groundwork of St. Matthew's. Thus, if we take the entry prior to the autumn communion of 1847, we find that it contains no fewer than 75 names, and includes certificates from Abbotshall, Arbroath, Bothwell, Brechin, Bridge-of-Allan, Bridge-of-Weir, Broughton, Campbeltown, Corstorphine, Crieff, Doune, Dundee,

Edinburgh, Govan, Greenock, Haddington, Helensburgh, Ireland, Johnstone, Kenmore, Kilmaurs, Kirkintilloch, Kirkmichael, Liverpool, Logierait, Manchester, Monifieth, Newton-on-Ayr, Partick, Perth, Renfrew, Troon, besides some from other city congregations of various denominations. These numerous accessions by certificate were quickly followed by large additions of young communicants, and it is worthy of note in passing, with what care Mr. Miller dealt with these, usually expecting also a report from the elder of the district to which they belonged. As the natural consequence of such expansion, repeated elections of elders and deacons had to be called for, and no fewer than four ordinations to each office took place during the short period we are now considering.

It very soon became evident that the church in Kent Road, which had so lately called forth the plaudits of the *Scottish Guardian*, was utterly inadequate for the requirements of the congregation. Within a year of Mr. Miller's settlement, the Deacons' Court had to pass a resolution to let sittings only to such as were without other place of worship, and to reserve certain pews exclusively for those who were aged, infirm, or dull of hearing. In December, 1845, the clerk reported "that the remaining seats had been let to *stated hearers*, all those who had sittings in other churches, and who used St. Matthew's merely as a convenience, being excluded." The pressure of new applications had been so great, however, that the Deacons had been unable to adhere to their own resolution as to reserving seats, but "hoped, by next term, when the remainder of the irregular sitters leave the church, to be in a position to reserve pews for those persons whose infirmities required their being near the pulpit." In 1848 the seat-letting committee again reported that very many applicants had been disappointed, in consideration whereof it was resolved "to open the false door from the church into the school-room, which would accommodate from fifty to sixty additional sitters."

In these circumstances it is small wonder that the question of a new church became one of urgent importance. Mr. Buchanan again figures as the untiring convener of a committee appointed to take prompt action, and in December, 1849, he was able to report its unanimous opinion in favour of "a site on the proposed continuation of Bath Street, and on the south side of that street, facing the centre of the new street which is being opened up from Sauchiehall Street, and right opposite the west corner of Albany Place." This last item in the definition is a manifest allusion to the proximity of Mr. Miller's own residence, which was then at No. 12 Albany Place, looking almost directly down Newton Street, and now covered by Charing Cross Mansions.

Designs were forthwith submitted by seven architects, and after due consideration that of Messrs. Black & Salmon was selected. The estimated cost came to £5750, exclusive of site, for which £1523 had already been paid, being at the rate of 23s. per square yard.

By March, 1850, £3500 of this had been subscribed, while it was assumed that a further £1200 might fairly be expected from the sale of the old church. "Your committee are confident," so runs their report, "that before the end of five years (over which subscriptions extend) all the debt will be liquidated. . . . Not more than seven years ago only 63 members joined themselves together as a congregation here, and now see how we have increased! (to 740). . . . Surely the building of a new church is not so arduous an undertaking as some imagine, with such prospects as we have before us now." Little did the sanguine convener foresee that before all was done the expenditure would mount up to nearly £13,500, or that, with accumulated interest, the burden would not be entirely removed for thirty years to come.

No time was now lost in proceeding with the work, and on the seventh day of August the foundation stone was happily laid. The following documents, contained in a sealed bottle, were deposited in it :

1. Assembly papers with reference to new church.
2. Names of Members of Session and Deacons' Court.
3. Names of Members of Finance and Building Committees.
4. Names of Architects, Clerk of Works, and Tradesmen.
5. Extracts from relative Minutes of Deacons' Court.

6. Authoritative exposition of Free Church principles, as contained in The Pastoral Address, Claim of Right, Protest, Act of Separation, and Deed of Demission.

7. Catechism on the Principles and Constitution of the Free Church of Scotland.

8. *Home and Foreign Record*, and *Children's Missionary Record* of the Free Church of Scotland for August, 1850.

9. *Free Church Magazine* for August, 1850.

10. Copy of *Scottish Guardian* for 6th August, and copies of *Witness* and *Daily Mail* for 7th August, 1850.

11. Statement on Post Office question by Sabbath Alliance.

12. Medal of the late Rev. Dr. Chalmers, commemorative of the Disruption.

A study of the records of the time impresses one with the conviction that this was the heroic age of deacons' courts. While these heavy drafts were being made in connection with local church and school building, constant appeals were likewise coming in from Dr. Buchanan as to the Sustentation Fund and new Normal Seminary; from Dr. Guthrie as to the Manse Fund; from Dr. Candlish as to the Education Fund; from Dr. James Buchanan as to the Foreign Mission Building Fund; from Dr. Begg as to the

General Building Fund; besides from many
other quarters. To these the court always lent
a willing ear, and usually extended a generous
hand. Before the congregation of St. Matthew's attended to their own comfort in the
matter of a new church, they were actually
contributing between £1000 and £1200 to
the general Sustentation Fund, and were thus
practically maintaining a gospel ministry in
seven or eight less favoured localities. We
do not record this by way of congregational
glorification, or in forgetfulness of the fact
that St. Matthew's then occupied an altogether exceptional position in the expanding
metropolis of the west, but rather as an
actual and vivid illustration of obedience to
certain scriptural injunctions, more heartily
realized, perhaps, in those days than in our
own. "Bear ye one another's burdens, and
so fulfil the law of Christ" (Gal. vi. 2).
"Look not every man on his own things,
but every man also on the things of others"
(Phil. ii. 4).

It may be a fitting conclusion to this chapter if we here mention that it was in July,
1848, that Mr. Miller received the degree

of D.D. from Princeton College, America.
The honour came unexpectedly, and was
appropriately conveyed to him by letter from
another Samuel Miller, D.D., then an octo-
genarian professor in that institution, who had
all along manifested a keen interest in the
Free Church movement. It reached and
cheered him at a time when he was tem-
porarily laid aside by illness, and it need
hardly be said that a wide circle beyond his
own congregation rejoiced in the distinction
thus worthily conferred.

IV

Dr. Miller's Ministry
1851-65

"When the Lord shall build up Zion, He shall appear in His glory."

PSALM cii. 16.

Dr. Miller's Ministry
1851-65

THE 12th of October, 1851, was a day of
gladness of heart to the people of St.
Matthew's. On that autumn morning—just
seven years from the coming of Dr. Miller—
their second temple was solemnly dedicated.
The zealous anxiety of the office-bearers was
at length rewarded, and the dream of years was
realized. A brief minute, dated 22nd October,
runs as follows : " The Session, grateful to
Almighty God for all the way by which He
has led them, and that by His good hand upon
them, the congregation have been enabled to
erect for themselves a more commodious place
of worship, consider it proper to put on record
at this place that the new church was opened

for divine worship on the twelfth day of this month." The following account of the memorable services is from the *Scottish Guardian*:

OPENING OF FREE ST. MATTHEW'S CHURCH.

"The new church, erected by the congregation of the Rev. Dr. Samuel Miller, and situated in the new prolongation of Bath Street, fronting Newton Street, Sauchiehall Road, was opened for public worship on Sabbath last. The services were conducted, in the forenoon by the Rev. Dr. Duff (Moderator of the General Assembly), in the afternoon by Rev. Dr. Miller, and in the evening by Rev. Dr. Buchanan. All the discourses were of a very impressive description, and were attended by crowded audiences. The collection at the three diets amounts to the munificent sum of £752 10s. This edifice is the most graceful of our Free Church structures in Glasgow. The style of architecture is decorated English, after designs by Messrs. Black & Salmon. The flanks of the church are finished with embattled parapets and buttresses, and the windows are embellished with elaborate stone tracery. The pulpit window is 28 feet high by 12½ feet wide, and the glass of all the windows has been stained in a style of great taste and beauty by Mr. Ballantyne of Edinburgh. The front of the church is ornamented with a tower terminating in a spire, which rises to a height of 200 feet, being consequently the highest spire in Glasgow, with the exception of that of the Cathedral. The tower is furnished with richly crocketed pinnacles, and from the general variety of surface, and beauty of outline, the effect of light and shade is very beautiful. The interior has a light and airy appearance, and is well ventilated. We congratulate

Stuart, Glasgow

FIFE ST. MATTHEW'S CHURCH.

this highly respectable and influential congregation on the erection of an edifice so much better suited to their comfort· and accommodation than the one they have left, and which adds an architectural ornament to the west end of the city. A fine toned bell has been placed in the tower, and is to be accompanied by a clock, both of which will prove a public benefit to that rapidly improving neighbourhood."

The collection was a remarkable one for those or any other days, and, with the small deduction of £7 10s. for ordinary expenses, the entire sum was devoted to the Building Fund.

This thing, not having been done in a corner, created considerable talk over the country, and was not without its lesson and stimulus. Dr. Duff had a story of how an Episcopalian congregation in England, comprising fifteen hundred worshippers, used effusively to welcome the annual deputation from the Church Missionary Society, and how after the customary sermons had been preached, they were wont to announce that the "handsome" sum of £6 or £7 had been taken up. When some of those well-to-do people were shown the paragraph stating that £752 had been got at a Glasgow Free Church collection they simply refused to believe it, insisting that the printer had added an extra figure at the beginning or end; it must be either £75 or £52, though both seemed alike incredible.

Yet this was by no means the record collection of those times. When Free St. John's was opened in 1845, the sum of £1778 14s. 11¼d. was put into the plate. On that occasion Dr. Chalmers was the preacher, and, as it turned out, it was also his last appearance in a Glasgow pulpit. His texts were, "Take heed what ye hear," and "Take heed how ye hear." Dr. Merle d'Aubigné, happening to be of the audience, has thus recorded his impressions in a volume entitled *Recollections of a Swiss Minister*. "The crowds," he says, "gathered from all quarters, but you can have no idea of the order and the devotion of the assembly. On leaving the church, Chalmers took my arm, and we retired together. It was with difficulty we could make our way along. The 40,000 francs thrown into the plate by Christians, who to build this church had already taxed themselves extraordinarily, is a characteristic feature of the Free Church of Scotland."

Men's hearts had not till then been really opened to the needs of the world, or to a sense of individual responsibility, even in the poor measure of our own day. As Dr. Thomas Brown truly says, " The fountain of Christian liberality needed to be broken up, and, in the providence of God, this was what the Disruption was sent to do. Under the quickening power of the Spirit of God, men's hearts were enlarged, and they began to give of their substance as they never gave before. The first outburst of this liberality was wonderful ; but more wonderful is the fact, that it proved to be no temporary convulsive effort. The generous impulse became a habit."

Such a *habit* was indeed very necessary in the case of St. Matthew's, for what with simultaneous outlay on church and school, inevitable under-estimates, and accumulating interest, debt had already assumed alarming proportions. In the year 1852 this untoward item stood in the treasurer's books at £11,444. Part had, no doubt, been subscribed, and was being paid by instalments, but the greater portion was quite unprovided for. It was nevertheless strongly felt by the large-hearted office-bearers that, while gradual reduction was a duty to be steadily kept in view, the interests of the church at large must not in the meantime be allowed to suffer. In this very year when local burdens were at a maximum, no less a sum than £1108 was remitted to the Central Sustentation Fund. Three years later the sum of £1372 was sent in, and in 1858 this was increased to £1406. Dr. Miller was all this time content with a modest supplement, while setting an example of generosity by an annual contribution to the Building Fund.

In these brave days patriotic Deacons' Courts thought it a small matter to tax even congregational income, that they might more liberally aid the common good. Perhaps they are now too complacently satisfied if total revenue is on the ascending scale, without sufficiently regarding how it has been raised or how distributed. Is there not some danger of so constantly pressing for increased ordinary collections as to obscure the higher aims of our Christian association, and of so dealing with the commercial aspects of seat-letting as to discourage some from joining whom we ought specially to welcome? There seems need also that a watchful jealousy should be exercised over the frequency of presentations, the promiscuous sale of tickets by church societies, and the collecting from all and sundry for superfluous congregational luxuries, lest too large a proportion of what has been "laid by in store," as the Lord's portion, should be diverted from worthier objects. It surely remains one of the most important functions of a Deacons' Court, to give wise *direction* to the liberality of the people, and very specially to secure that the great central Sustentation and Foreign Mission Funds—so ably managed at headquarters for five and fifty years—shall hold the first place in their hearts. On these two funds depend the very existence and utility of our church, and they unquestionably afford the best channels for effective help from our smaller givers.

From this digression we return to notice the means that were adopted to remove the great incubus of debt resting on the congregation. In March, 1853, a special committee reported fresh subscriptions to the amount of £3525, spread over five years. In 1856 the

old church in Kent Road was sold to the
Free West congregation, who had for a time
rented it, thus bringing in £1300. Again,
early in 1859, ten members offered to make
up £1000 during the next five years, provided the remaining membership raised the
sum of £1500. This cost an effort, which
for a time threatened to be just barely successful; but, in November, the Finance Committee reported, "that the entire sum of
£1500 had now been subscribed, fulfilling the
condition on which the £1000 was contributed, by ten members, and making in all
£2500." By March, 1864, the large debt
was thus reduced to £2853. In that year a
fresh movement was inaugurated, £1600 being
subscribed, payable over a couple of years, so
that in 1866 we find it had melted to £1399.
Efforts were thereafter considerably relaxed,
and, in 1870, the sum of £880 was still outstanding. Ten years later, owing to adverse
circumstances which supervened, this amount
had been allowed to increase by a couple of
hundred pounds, so that to Dr. Miller it was
never given to see his loved St. Matthew's
entirely free of debt. That the balance did

not, however, remain indefinitely against the congregation, will be seen from a subsequent chapter.

In December, 1856, the Presbytery of Glasgow selected three of the elders—Messrs. Andrew Nielson, T. L. Paterson, and John Thomson—to act as assessors in Finnieston church, then being formed into a territorial charge under the ministry of Rev. Andrew A. Bonar of Collace, till such time as a regular Session of its own could be chosen. Mr. Nielson, with the hearty approbation of Dr. Miller, ultimately resolved to remain with the new congregation, and became its first Session-clerk. His experience and zeal were sorely missed at the time, but the generosity of St. Matthew's, in then parting with so valuable an office-bearer, was in later years repaid by the reception into its own Session of a worthy son of this worthy father.

In the anxious endeavour to curtail expenditure at the outset, the hall below the church had been left uncompleted. If the homely accommodation it has now for so long afforded still leaves something to be desired, it is not amiss to remember that for five or six years we had to get along without anything. The interesting manner in which this boon was at length acquired, and the pleasure with which it was welcomed, are vividly brought before us in the minute of Deacons' Court for 9th February, 1857:

"Mr. Forrester, chairman of committee, invited the Court to inspect the premises below the church and to accept them, now completed, as a gift to the Deacons' Court and congregation. The Court, having made this inspection, unanimously expressed their satisfaction and delight at the substantial and elegant manner in which the work has been accomplished, and their grateful acceptance of the valuable addition thus made to the kirk fabric for the accommodation of the congregation. Dr. Miller, in name of the whole Court, returned thanks to Mr. Forrester, and the young men of whom he has been the organ in all this matter, for the energy and self-sacrificing enterprise with which they have brought their spirited undertaking to so satisfactory a conclusion, at an outlay of £264 16s. 6d., which has been met and defrayed by their own personal exertions. And farther, the Deacons' Court unanimously resolved thus to record this well-earned tribute of their gratitude in the minutes of this sederunt; and as Mr. Allan, the clerk of Court, has been one of those who have been most forward in this labour of love, they requested the Moderator and Mr. Paul to relieve him from the duty of sounding the praises of himself and his associates by preparing a draft of this minute to be engrossed on the record;—which they hereby have done accordingly."

It appears that, by almost unpardonable

thoughtlessness, the windows on both sides of the church, as well as at the tower end had, in conformity with some whim of the day, been painted over, with the result described by Elihu of old, that "men saw not the bright light which was in the clouds." By-and-by, with the added dust of years, it seemed as if a perpetual fog had settled down upon the worshippers. In 1860 Mr. T. L. Paterson is reported as complaining, at the Deacons' Court, with a touch of grim humour, that the "light was inefficient, making the church so dark and uncomfortable that several parties were likely to leave in consequence, while others, particularly the young, were unwilling to come to such a dark and dismal church." The advice of Mr. Burnet, architect, having been taken, and several experiments having been tried, the obnoxious paint was ordered to be removed by a powerful acid,—at considerable expense.

The Day School at Anderston continued to receive the most conscientious and painstaking oversight from the office-bearers, and in 1858 we find Mr. Nielson reporting increased prosperity, 300 children being then in attendance. The annual examination had just taken place, when the children acquitted themselves to the satisfaction of the inspectors and of a large number of visitors.

In 1860 the Presbytery granted leave to dispense the communion at the Mission, and, on the recommendation of Mr. Christison, missionary, nineteen persons were admitted to membership there, thus forming the original nucleus of what was to be afterwards known as Cranstonhill Free Church. From that date forward the ordinance continued to be celebrated half-yearly in the same place.

In the winter of 1862-63 much distress from scarcity of employment prevailed in the district, especially among mill-girls. Into the task of relieving this misery Mrs. Miller and a committee of ladies threw themselves with characteristic ardour. Sewing was taught and paid for at the rate of sixpence a day; and a basin of warm soup (often supplied gratis by Mr. Corbett, of Cooking Depot fame), with a halfpenny worth of bread, was given to as many as possible. At the close of the effort, Mrs. Miller detailed as under how £90 voted by the Deacons' Court had been expended, viz. :

Wages paid to girls, - - - -	£63	4 6
Materials, not otherwise contributed, -	6	7 0
Soup tickets, - - - - -	4	10 6
Bread, - - - - - - -	3	8 0
Teacher, - - - - - -	8	8 0
Balance on hand, - - - -	4	2 0
	£90	0 0

Whereupon the Court requested Mrs. Miller to retain the balance as stated, for behoof of a poor member who had been mentioned.

Meantime the wear and tear of fifteen busy years had told seriously upon the Mission premises which served so many purposes from Sunday to Saturday, but how to raise the necessary funds to put them in proper order was a question of some difficulty. In May, 1863, however, this was completely solved by Mr. Allan, who handed in to the Deacons' Court duly receipted accounts for the complete overhaul of the school buildings, amounting to £319 16s., which he had raised entirely by private subscription. It is little wonder that we find this Court awarding a special vote of thanks to the committee for carrying out and collecting funds for such a praiseworthy object; and, farther, expressing their deep obligation to Mr. Allan for the great personal labour and attention he had bestowed on the work.

The Annual Social Meeting of the congregation was a great event in those days. That of 1852, for example—the first after the acquisition of the present church—was held in the City Hall, 1000 persons being present; and was addressed by Rev. Drs. Miller and Buchanan, Revs. William Arnot and George Wisely, and Professor Miller from Edinburgh. The sum of £55 9s. 10d. was collected at the door, "being fully equal to the expenses incurred." It was afterwards generally found more convenient to hold these gatherings either in the church or in the Queen's Rooms.

At an early point in the congregational history, it was felt by many that the service of praise was anything but worthily rendered, and efforts were made from time to time to improve the practice in this respect. As early as 1845 the precentor had to be "communicated with on the subject of his inefficiency." He was rather taken by surprise in the matter, "being quite satisfied with his own performances," but the Deacons' Court, adhering to their view, proceeded to advertise for another leader. In 1846 the new precentor asked the use of a piano for his weekly exercises. He estimated the expense at £3 to £4, but anticipated great advantage to follow. The minute bears that, "after discussion, the request was granted upon the express condition that the instrument was to be kept in the school-room, and at no time to be brought into the church."

In 1854 a communication was read from Dr. Brown of St. James's on the subject of Congregational Psalmody, asking that representatives might be chosen to act on a Presbyterial Committee, whereupon Messrs. Sprunt, Allan, and Church were appointed. In 1855 this committee recommended the formation of district classes for the improvement of psalmody, and the Deacons' Court agreed to allow the use of the church for the northwest district, comprising St. George's, St. Enoch's, St. Stephen's, St. Matthew's, Milton, and Maryhill, "provided the expense of lighting, heating, cleaning, and attendance be defrayed by the committee."

In the latter part of 1862, we find the Con-

E

gregational Psalmody Committee asking that
four pews in front of the pulpit be devoted
to the accommodation of "a number of the
congregation, who have agreed to sit together
with the view of assisting the precentor in
leading the music during divine service," and
early in the following year this petition was
also complied with. About the same date a
meeting was convened of all in the congregation interested in the subject of psalmody,
when "it was agreed, without dissent, to form
a class of such as possessed sufficient musical
qualification to enable them at once to sing in
parts." The class was formed under the
tuition of Julius Seligmann, a still surviving
professor of the art, and it is specially stated
that it was regarded as essential that the
precentor should also be present, and co-
operate generally in the new departure.

In carrying out even these small changes
with the view of promoting harmonious praise,
it will be noted how carefully the higher harmony of the congregation was safeguarded.
Were office-bearers always to act in the same
spirit—guiding, by all means, yet never an-
ticipating, and still less forcing the general

sentiment—how much painful heartburning would be saved! There are purposes for which majorities are not sufficient, but where practical unanimity is essential. All things may indeed be lawful, but all things are not expedient.

A singular fact which has to be noticed is the frequency with which cases of discipline came before the Session. This state of things continued for the first twenty years of our existence as a congregation, after which such cases all at once became as rare as they happily are to-day. How far this curious phenomenon is to be accounted for by the extraordinary influx of strangers St. Matthew's had to deal with at the beginning, or how far to a lower view then prevalent as to the obligations of church membership, it is now hard to say.

During the period embraced by the present chapter the Session were called on to mourn the loss by death of several of their number who seemed to be pillars, and beautiful tributes to their memory, in which we can often trace the deft hand of Dr. Miller, were engrossed on the record. In 1849, there passed away Robert Fleming, " a worthy

elder, a Christian citizen, a brother beloved";
in 1855, Hugh Cogan, "a Christian gentleman
of unostentatious but devoted piety"; in 1860,
James Wright, "a beloved friend and most
efficient elder"; in 1861, Allan Buchanan, "to
whom it was not a little owing that the congregation maintained its individual existence
at the time of the Disruption"; on 19th May,
1862, Alexander Wingate, "a man of sterling
worth and great modesty, of steadfast principle and guileless simplicity, of singularly
blameless life and tender heart"; and on the
very same day, John Wilson, "a father in
Israel. . . . These were lovely in their lives,
and in their death not divided"; in 1864,
David Stow, "a man whose name will be
honoured, and whose memory will be blessed
for generations to come in connection with
the godly upbringing of the young"; and
in 1865, William Paul, "much esteemed and
loved." These all died in faith, leaving
behind them fragrant memories and high
examples of simple trust in Jesus, and of
love to their fellowmen.

On the other hand the Session had twice
occasion to record "their grateful thanks to

God for His kindness to them and to the congregation in restoring to health their esteemed minister," after serious illnesses in 1852 and 1862. They had also frequent cause to acknowledge the services rendered by Dr. Buchanan, Dr. Smyth, and Mr. Arnot, in the capacity of interim moderators. In later years such duties were frequently discharged by the Rev. Principal Douglas, D.D., who was ever ready to give any assistance in his power to the minister or people of St. Matthew's.

V

Dr. Miller's Ministry
1866-81

"They shall see eye to eye, when the Lord shall bring again Zion."

ISAIAH lii. 8.

Dr. Miller's Ministry
1866-81

IN the latter part of 1866 a wide-spread fear existed lest an outbreak of cholera might occur in our city. A committee, presided over by the Lord Provost, took energetic action, by sub-dividing the poorer neighbourhoods, and allocating these to the supervision of responsible local bodies. To the congregation of Free St. Matthew's was naturally allotted its own Mission District in Anderston, and Mr. Wyper undertook the organization of visitors. On the 12th November he was able to inform the Deacons' Court that the entire district assigned to the congregation had been overtaken, and that the visitors' reports had already been sent in to the Sanitary Office. So

efficiently indeed had the work been carried
through, that the authorities asked him to supervise an additional district west of the church,
bounded by North Street, Kent Road, Kelvin-
haugh Street and Sauchiehall Street, "but,"
says the report, "in the respectable parts of
this district, it was not considered necessary
to do more than employ a man to deliver
tracts, containing the recommendations of the
Sanitary Committee." The matter again came
before the Court in the following year, but
no action seems to have been called for.

A wholesome dread of "germs" had, however, taken possession of the members, for,
when the ladies asked for the use of one of
the rooms below the church to hold their
society's wardrobe, the application was refused
on the ground "that it was considered danger-
ous to have the recipients of their charity
coming about the church." A month later
the ladies returned to the charge, pleading
"that the room was wanted simply for stor-
ing the clothing, and not for dispensing it,"
whereupon a future Lord Provost, now Sir
John Muir, Bart., moved, and it was agreed,
"that the use of the room under the vestry

be granted for this purpose." Before the year was out, however, the dauntless ladies once more applied for "the use of the room not merely as a store-room, but also for dispensing the clothing, on the understanding that entry would be made only from the lane behind the church," which was finally conceded; nor did any evil effects follow.

In 1868, on a report given in by Mr. Gilbert Beith, afterwards M.P. for the Central Division and for Inverness-shire, the Boys' and Girls' Schools, which had hitherto been distinct, were amalgamated in terms of a new Education code, and placed under the general management of a headmaster, with a lady assistant for the junior department. A cordial vote of thanks was at the same time awarded to Mrs. Miller and the other ladies who had organized and so long efficiently superintended the operations of the female school, and an earnest desire was expressed for a continuance of the same hearty interest in the amalgamated school. From this time forward there is no more prominent item of Deacons' Court business than the very full quarterly reports on the working of this large undertaking, particulars being regularly furnished as to the number of boys and girls on the roll, the average attendance in each department, the exact number transferred from the junior to the senior section, and an account of the fees drawn. Messrs. Allan, Connell, Hay, and M'Kill seem to have successively held the laborious office of convener for lengthy periods, until the prosperous school was finally transferred to the School Board in 1883. At the examination of 1868 we notice that specimens of the pupils' drawing, maps, and penmanship, together with a quantity of varied and excellent industrial work were exhibited. The Rev. Alexander Whyte of St. John's (now of St. George's, Edinburgh, and Moderator of this year's General Assembly) gave an admirable address, and prizes were presented by friends in the congregation.

In 1872 the Session were gratified by receiving proposals from Mr. John C. Gibson, now missionary in Swatow, and other students, offering active co-operation in the work of the Mission. This led to fuller consideration of the methods then in use, with the result that the Session agreed to divide the whole ground into twelve small districts, with an elder, a student, and a mission member in charge of each, the elder and student to conduct a weekly kitchen meeting within their bounds, and the mission member to co-operate with ladies from St. Matthew's in visitation.

In the same year the Mission Committee reported that, in their opinion, the time had come for the procuring of more comfortable premises, and that a suitable site was obtainable in Cranston Street at about 21s. per square yard. They added that a hall to seat 400 would cost £1200, or a plain church to seat 800, about £2400.

Efforts were immediately made to ascertain how far such a movement would meet with sympathetic response in the congregation, and an application for a grant was at the same time forwarded to the Glasgow Church-building Fund. In a few months the committee farther reported that the site had been provisionally secured, that they believed £2000 might be reckoned on from the congregation, and that the Building Society had promised £500 towards a hall, or £1500 towards a

church. Designs for both were obtained, but,
as it turned out that a larger plot of
ground than was actually needful had to be
purchased, it was found impossible to con-
template more than the smaller scheme for
the present. On Sabbath, 9th November,
1873, a nice hall was opened, and at a
subsequent meeting of Deacons' Court much
thankfulness was expressed that so commodious and convenient a building had been
erected for the Mission congregation, free of
debt, and that the reports of the various
agencies were so satisfactory.

In due time the Presbytery sanctioned the
erection of the preaching station into a
regular mission charge, under the name of
Cranstonhill Free Church. On 22nd February, 1877, the congregation worshipping there
resolved to invite the Rev. Alexander Linn
of St. Fergus, a former missionary, to become
their minister, and 116 members and 70
adherents signed the call. On the 14th
May Mr. Linn was inducted, and remains
pastor to this day. St. Matthew's thus found
itself relieved of the spiritual oversight of this
people, and shortly afterwards closed its official

connection with Cranstonhill by handing over to the minister a sum of £416 8s., being the balance collected towards the ultimate erection of a church. Dr. Miller at the same time drew up a statement commending this new cause to the Free Church public.

Turning now to the congregation itself, we find that the Sustentation Fund continued to receive the most painstaking attention under the convenership of Mr. F. J. Ferguson, who held that post for twenty years. In January, 1867, the Deacons' Court adopted certain recommendations of his committee, some of which it may not be amiss to reproduce even to-day. We quote the following :

"That where deacons are not themselves the ordinary collectors, they should hold themselves responsible for seeing that the collections are regularly gathered in, and that they themselves should visit each his own district at least twice a year, and on these occasions receive the contributions personally.

"That in making their half-yearly visits, they should confer with the people, where it is thought reasonable, as to the propriety of increasing their contributions, and also deal with non-contributors as to the duty and privilege of contributing to the Lord's cause ; due regard being had to cases of delicacy and difficulty.

"That with the view of increasing the mutual interest of

deacon and collector in their respective districts, your committee farther suggests that previous to the monthly contributions being given in, the deacon compare the slip with his collector's book, initial the slip, and hand it in with the money to the treasurer.

"Your committee consider the sum of £1300 a reasonable amount for this congregation to contribute."

As showing what may be accomplished by a judicious visitation, it was reported, about a year later, that an aggregate increase might be expected of £141 9s. 4d. On the occasion of another similar effort, the increase was even greater. The number of individual subscribers at this time was 397; it is now, as we learn from last report, 580. In 1870, we notice that a tendency was exhibited in some quarters to withhold contributions because of divided counsels in the church on the subject of union, but the watchful Deacons' Court promptly deprecated such unreasonable action. For twenty-six years from the opening of the second Free St. Matthew's an average of £1284 was maintained — a really splendid record. The high water mark of £1481 was touched in 1875.

We have referred to the length of service rendered by Mr. F. J. Ferguson in one de-

partment of congregational work. A glance
at the appendix will show that such persever-
ance in duty has been characteristic of St.
Matthew's throughout. Dr. Miller, indeed, led
the way by an unusually prolonged ministry,
but it ought to be specially recorded, that for
thirty years the minutes of session are engrossed in a single handwriting—Mr. Wm.
Cumming having held the office of Clerk from
1846 to 1876. In like manner Mr. Wm.
Church acted as Congregational Treasurer for
three-and-twenty years, and several others
have closely emulated these examples.

In the summers of 1867 and 1868, the congregation united for two or three months
with the College Church, each worshipping
for half the time in the edifice of the other.
On both occasions Dr. Miller was laid aside
by illness, his place being supplied in the latter
year by the Rev. J. R. Elder, son of the
venerated Dr. Elder of Rothesay. In 1869
the church was thoroughly overhauled at an
outlay of £600, and in 1877 it was again re-
paired and cleaned at an expenditure of £450.

It will be remembered that, from 1863 to 1873,
negotiations for union with the United Pres-

byterian and Reformed Presbyterian Churches
were in progress. While at first all promised
well, differences of opinion by-and-by manifested themselves, which became greatly accen-
tuated in the later years. The controversy
invaded all the courts of our church, nor was
the Session of St. Matthew's by any means
exempt. While Dr. Miller, who had the
friendliest relations with all the churches, did
not conceal his strong antipathy to the idea
of incorporating union, a majority of the elders
were keenly in favour of it. This led to a
strained state of feeling which revealed itself
in a variety of ways, trying to both sections
of the Court. It had, for instance, been the
happy use and wont, as it still is, to choose
the half-yearly representative to the Presbytery in strict rotation; but when it came to
be a question of grave moment how each
vote should count in critical divisions, the
majority insisted on their legal right to
nominate a member of their own party.
This unusual step led to dissents with elaborate reasons attached, which in turn required
answers, and so the thing went on from year
to year. At length, in its wisdom, the

Assembly of 1873 saved the whole church from rupture by abandoning the negotiations altogether, till such time as brethren might be able to see more nearly eye to eye.

An earnest of the good time then foreshadowed was happily realised, when in 1876 the Reformed Presbyterian Church united with our own, enriching our evangelical succession with her Goolds, her Symingtons, her Binnies, and everything now points to an early consummation of the larger union originally contemplated. May we not even hope that the day is at hand, when all, who from different stand-points have longed and laboured for a united, yet spiritually independent Presbyterianism, shall be gathered into one!

The painful differences, to which we have alluded, were a severe strain upon Dr. Miller's sensitive, if somewhat imperious nature, and in the winters of the two following years he was compelled to seek a more genial climate for several months together. Minutes of affectionate sympathy followed him to Cannes, as well as letters keeping him abreast of St. Matthew's news, while in return there were received, from time to time, pastoral letters of great beauty and tenderness, which were eagerly read and highly valued.

Meanwhile, it had become evident that, both for Dr. Miller's sake and for the sake of the congregation, it was desirable that a colleague should be associated in the work of the ministry. The attitude of Dr. Miller was admirable. Unable, through illness, to be present at the first congregational meeting called to consider the matter, he wrote:

"Let me entreat you not to fetter the conscientious freedom of your choice by considerations of how I may be affected thereby. . . . It is from God you must ask the man whom He shall choose. . . . I shall indeed give thanks and rejoice to be associated with such a brother. May he and I and you be blessed of God together."

Overtures were in course of time made to the Rev. John Chalmers, M.A., of Arbroath, and to the Rev. John M. Sloan, M.A., of Aberdeen; but unanimity not being obtained, proceedings in both cases fell to the ground. It was, indeed, apparent that the cleavage of feeling which had developed during the union controversy was still interfering to a great extent with the remarkable harmony which had prevailed in former years.

At length the air was cleared, but by a disruption alas!—equally painful, it is believed, to those who separated themselves and to those who remained. In the autumn of 1876 eleven elders and nine deacons judged it their duty to demit office at meetings of Session held in Dr. Miller's house. Efforts were made to alter the decision they had arrived at, but as these proved unavailing, the Session had sorrowfully to record the severance of their official and congregational connection with St. Matthew's. In doing so the good work accomplished by many of them was fully recognized, and the hope was expressed " that wherever they might go the presence of the Lord might go with them."

Those were indeed dark days for St. Matthew's,—with Dr. Miller in feeble health, a dismembered session and strained finances; yet, having paid this just tribute to departed comrades, the remaining elders, after installing Mr. Thomas Wharrie as Session-clerk, like brave men at once buckled on their armour, and prepared for a forward march. Large reinforcements of elders and deacons were speedily called for, voted, and brought into

line. And so it came to pass, under the over-
ruling providence of God, that while other
congregations were enriched by valuable accessions, St. Matthew's not only held on its
way, but was enabled to enter with some
faith upon ever-expanding opportunities of
service. In less than a year the Rev. John
Watson, M.A., was happily settled as co-
pastor, a circumstance which proved an im-
mense relief both to Dr. Miller and to the
office-bearers. New mission work was thereafter undertaken in the north-west district, for
which funds were readily forthcoming, but of
this enterprise we shall speak more fully when
we come to deal with Mr. Watson's ministry.

In November, 1879, a great gathering in
Dr. Miller's honour was held in the Queen's
Rooms. He was on that occasion surrounded
by a galaxy of past, present and prospective
moderators, as well as by other notabilities.
Amongst those present were the Revs. Sir
H. W. Moncrieff, D.D., Principal Douglas,
D.D., J. C. Burns, D.D., Thomas Smith,
D.D., A. A. Bonar, D.D., Robert Elder, D.D.,
John Adam, D.D., Thomas M'Lauchlan, D.D.,
Thomas Main (D.D.), Messrs. James Campbell

ANDREW NIELSON.

JOHN WILSON.

THOMAS WHARRIE,
Session Clerk, 1877-1887.

LAURENCE ROBERTSON.

JAMES M'MICHAEL.

of Tullichewan, and William M'Kinnon of
Ballinakill. Mr. Watson took the chair, and
in his happiest manner introduced the business of the evening. After gracefully alluding
to the higher qualities of head and heart
which characterized Dr. Miller, he concluded
by expressing the hope "that he was not
going beyond the bounds of good taste in
saying that many of them looked with a
kindly and admiring eye upon Dr. Miller's
personal appearance, and had a pardonable
anxiety that art should preserve to another
generation that form which they believed to
be the very index of the nobility of his
soul." Mr. Wharrie then presented Dr.
Miller, in name of numerous subscribers in
and out of the congregation, with that excellent portrait by Patalano, which has now,
in accordance with Mrs. Miller's will, become
the property of the Free Church College.

Within a year Mr. Watson, to the great
grief of all, was unexpectedly translated to
another sphere. While thus plunged in the
uncertainties of a vacancy, the office-bearers
were cheered by the receipt of an excerpt
from the trust disposition and settlement

of a member of the congregation, directing
her trustees to set aside the sum of twenty-
five hundred pounds for the purpose of
founding a mission in connection with the
congregation of Free St. Matthew's. Anxiety
with regard to recently assumed responsibilities was thus set at rest, and in March,
1881, the Session recorded "their desire
to return thanks to God, who had put
into the heart of the late Miss Jamieson to
leave this handsome sum to His service,
knowing as they do how much her heart was
set upon serving Him, both in her person
and in her substance."

Two months later the Rev. C. A. Salmond,
M.A., was inducted to the colleagueship;
but it will presently be seen how short a
time Dr. Miller himself was spared after
this auspicious settlement.

During the years with which we have been
dealing the hand of death had ever and anon
been stretched forth upon the Session and
congregation. Amongst those taken from the
eldership we may mention, in 1866 Robert
Burns, "humble and cheerful as a Christian,
upright and honourable as a merchant, and

devotedly laborious as an elder"; also Robert Forrester, "for thirty years an elder, of solid judgment and enlarged experience"; in 1868 William Mirrlees, "one of those through whose zeal and energy the congregation was established at the Disruption"; also William Mac-Kinlay, "whose last Sabbath was spent in serving tables at the Lord's Supper here, and who was then taken to that table whereat Christ drinks the wine anew with His disciples in the upper sanctuary"; in 1871 Francis J. Ferguson, "conspicuous for his Christian worth and energy"; also James Macarthur, "the prominent features of whose character were simplicity and godly sincerity"; in 1872 John Duncan, "a man of singular worth and amiability, a faithful elder, a loving friend, and a humble-minded Christian"; in 1875 Robert B. Park, "whose humility covered an unostentatious zeal for his heavenly Father's glory, and for the welfare, temporal and spiritual, of God's poor"; and in 1876 David Hay, "a pre-Disruption elder, eminently useful and deservedly beloved alike by his brethren in office and by all the people."

Dr. Miller's own health, which had often

given cause for grave anxiety, at length broke down entirely. In April, 1881, he dispensed the Lord's Supper for the last time. In May he presided, in the best of spirits, at the reception given to his young colleague, but it proved to be also his farewell to his flock. At the meeting he caught a chill, from which he never rallied, and on the 5th of July he calmly fell asleep in Jesus. On the 8th a vast procession wended its way to the necropolis amid lines of deeply moved spectators, for it was known in Glasgow that "a prince and a great man had fallen." "Even so, Father, for so it seemed good in Thy sight. He has departed to be with Christ, which is far better. He has fought a good fight, he has finished his course, he has kept the faith. Henceforth there is laid up for him a crown of righteousness."

After quoting these last verses, the minute of Session, referring to their late pastor, proceeds :

"They remember with admiration his upright and open-hearted integrity as a man, and his unflinching rectitude and high honour as a churchman. They remember with affection the kindly interest in all the members of his flock, and specially the pastoral offices he so tenderly fulfilled among the sick, the dying and the bereaved. But above all do they remember, with gratitude, his supreme influence as a faithful and eloquent preacher of the Word, with which his own soul was so thoroughly imbued, and, they hereby put on record as the crowning feature of the service Dr. Miller rendered, and as that which constitutes the congregation's crowning responsibility in view of such a ministry— his sound and faithful exposition, and earnest and eloquent application of the truth of God, just as he found it in God's own Word, keeping back nothing that was profitable either for the correction of sinners or the edification of believers— not shunning to declare all the counsel of God, but making it his consistent aim rightly to divide the word of truth. There are many witnesses, living and departed, to the power under God, of Dr. Miller's pulpit ministrations; and the Session profoundly believe that only the day will declare how many there are who have had cause to bless God for sending them such a minister. He was a faithful minister of Christ, of the Church, and of the Word. He was a just man, and has joined the spirits of just men made perfect. He being dead yet speaketh."

On the Sabbath following Dr. Miller's death funeral sermons were preached in St. Matthew's by his old and valued friend, the Rev. Professor Smeaton, D.D., by his late colleague, the Rev. John Watson, and by his successor, the Rev. Charles A. Salmond. We cannot do better than close this chapter with an extract from the discriminating eulo-

gium of Mr. Watson, himself a hearer of
Dr. Miller for three years. He said :

"His preaching was not occupied in building up and
defending, one by one, a series of doctrines, though it left
you in no doubt regarding the doctrines of the day. It did
not turn, you will remember, on questions of authorship,
and dates, and language. It seldom took the form either
of a biographical or historical study. It did not deal very
directly with the practical details of duty or service. It
could hardly even be said to be, in the ordinary sense of
the word, expository preaching. It was unique. It was
the scriptural exposition of scripture, and, at the risk of
deepening our sorrow, must I recall to your minds the
manner of his preaching. You can never forget with what
solemnity he gave out his text, and with what clearness
he stated its relation to the context; how he stated his
heads and explained their meaning, and *then* appeared the
peculiar feature of his sermons. Holding up the truth he
wished to expound—holding it up as it were in one hand,
with the other he illuminated it before our eyes. Turning
over the leaves of his well-worn Bible he quoted now from
a book of Moses, now from the writings of a Prophet, now
from a Gospel, now from an Epistle, making rays of light
from every corner of Holy Scripture to converge on the
truth in hand, till what at first may have seemed unin-
teresting, or even unintelligible, became bright and beautiful in a light that came, not from the creeds and philosophies
of men, but, from the eternal Word of God. Such preaching—need I remind you?—required a scholarly knowledge
of the Scriptures in their original tongues, a mind trained
to thought and reflection, a hard and persevering study
of the Bible, and a very special unction of the Holy Ghost.

And it was because Dr. Miller was one of the best students of his day, and one of the most spiritually minded men you could meet in any day, that he was able, by the grace of God, to lead his people into the richest and most satisfying pastures of the Gospel. Other features less remarkable, only because they are more common among all evangelical ministers, were his reverence for the Holy Scripture ;—you remember how he used to say, 'Thus saith the Lord,' how sometimes he said, 'Isaiah saith, that is the Lord by the mouth of Isaiah '—you remember that ;—the honourable place he gave to the work of the Holy Ghost, and his constant reference in some part of his sermon to the atoning work of our Lord Jesus Christ; together with his wide-spread knowledge of the trials and temptations of God's people. His power was of the highest kind, due not to any affectation of manner,—his manner was his own, and none of us would have wished it different—nor to the lavish use of illustration,—though you know at a time he could employ one with great effect—you remember when he preached on 'Who can bring a clean thing out of an unclean?' and the illustrations he employed in that sermon, —nor to anything like a habit of strained and laboured eloquence,—though he was a master of the most beautiful English—but simply to the truth of God preached by one of His ablest, most faithful and devoted servants, who knew nothing but Christ, and Christ crucified.

But along with the preacher went the man, and you could never separate the one from the other. I shall not venture to speak about him as a Christian. That would be presumptuous on my part, but Dr. Miller *was* a man, and a *real* man, and here and now I say boldly he was one of the kindest and largest-hearted men that ever lived. You, who have been long his attached people, know that, but others who only saw him at a far distance did not always understand him. Everyone was obliged to respect his lofty and spiritual tone, but I have often been amazed and indignant at finding that many fancied him stern and hard. Perhaps it was not their blame. Perhaps they had met him when he was suffering very severe pain, or when he was condemning unrighteousness, or perhaps they had only heard a false report. At any rate, to suppose him such a man was a lamentable mistake. He was the best of friends. He was not ready to take offence at the conduct of his friends, or to make exacting claims on their kindness. He always thought well of those he loved, and would do them good at any cost. There was nothing mean or small about him. He gave everyone credit for honesty, and he was the perfection of honesty himself. He had the unsuspicious nature of a child, and the royal dignity of a king. His love for little children, whom he delighted to hold in his arms, was very great, and a more gracious picture I never saw than when that splendid-looking man folded to his breast an infant he had just baptized. His tenderness of voice and spirit when he visited the sick and sorrowful, his forbearance with foolish or forward people, his interest in all the lights and shadows of human life and his sympathy with the dumb creatures of God; his unworldliness, his incapability of anything like compromise or unworthy diplomacy, his sympathy with all good men and good work; of these and many other characteristics I might speak were it possible. One thing I cannot omit; he rejoiced in the success of any minister who was preaching Christ; and if any one proclaimed Christ from this pulpit, though it were the weakest sermon that ever came from a Christian's lips, he would thank him for it, *because* he had preached Christ."

Mr. Watson's Ministry
1877-80

" Be glad then, ye children of Zion, and rejoice in the Lord your God : for He hath given you the former rain moderately, and He will cause to come down for you the rain, the former rain, and the latter rain."

JOEL ii. 23.

Mr. Watson's Ministry
1877-80

WE must now go back to the evening of 16th May, 1877, when a meeting of the congregation was convened in the church to consider a report of their colleague committee, presented by Mr. Wharrie. It was then moved by Mr. Patrick Robertson, seconded by Mr. William Miller, and unanimously agreed, to present a hearty call to the Rev. John Watson, M.A., of Logiealmond, to become colleague and successor to the Rev. Dr. Miller. The following commissioners were appointed to prosecute the call before the Presbytery of Perth—from the Session, Dr. Miller, Messrs. M'Calman, Ramsay, Wharrie and White; from the Deacons' Court, Messrs. Buchanan, Grier-

G

son, Miller and Robertson ; and from the
congregation, Messrs. Grady, Hislop and Turn-
bull.

Logiealmond, better known to-day as Drum-
tochty—thanks to the genius of the man St.
Matthew's had chosen—is a quiet little Perth-
shire parish, lying mainly in a cross-country
glen, sufficiently removed from everyday traffic
to be self-contained, and productive, as will
now be generally admitted, of an amazing
variety of strongly marked types of character.
It has always had its "sermon-tasters," and has
enjoyed, indeed, quite an enviable reputation
for the independent discovery of pulpit talent.
For this distinction, however, it has had to
pay the unavoidable penalty of frequent in-
vasion by ecclesiastical raiders, from the north
and from the south.   On the present occasion
it was threatened from both quarters at once.
Though this combination of circumstances left
small hope for Logiealmond, St. Matthew's
was not unduly disquieted, for it was able to
recall a similar experience three and thirty
years before, when its way had been made
entirely prosperous.   The following brief account of the Presbytery's proceedings, taken

from the *Herald* of 19th July, discloses fairly
well the points and outcome of the situation :

"At a special meeting of the Free Church Presbytery of
Perth held yesterday, the consideration of two calls addressed to the Rev. John Watson of Logiealmond was
proceeded with. The one call was from St. John's congregation, Montrose, to be successor to Rev. Mr. Nixon ;
and the other from St. Matthew's congregation, Glasgow,
to be colleague to Rev. Dr. Miller. The call from Montrose was signed by 535 communicants, and 126 adherents,
and the call from Glasgow by 456 members, and 130
adherents. After commissioners from the congregations
interested had been heard, Mr. Watson expressed his conviction that the charge in Montrose was too important for a
clergyman of his limited experience, and he therefore had
decided to accept the call from Glasgow."

The Session minuted their thankfulness to
God for this favourable issue; and, as it seemed
desirable that Mr. Watson should have a short
respite before entering upon his new duties,
it was resolved to utilise the interval in re-
decorating the church.

On 13th September, the Presbytery of Glasgow met for Mr. Watson's induction, Mr. Ryrie
of Hutchesontown preaching and presiding.
The new minister received a cordial welcome
from his people, and on the following Sabbath

was formally introduced by his uncle, the Rev. Hiram Watson of Ratho. That much was expected from the new settlement is evident from the fact that, at the October communion, 52 persons joined St. Matthew's by certificate, considerable numbers being added at each succeeding occasion.

Although Mr. Watson's pastorate was not destined to be of long duration, an event occurred in the course of it which has had far-reaching results, not only to the congregational life of St. Matthew's, but to many beyond its pale. We refer to the commencement of mission work at Springbank, which took place under the following providential circumstances.

Early in 1879, a deputation of mission workers belonging to Free St. Stephen's waited upon the junior minister, and having informed him of the intention of their Session and Deacons' Court to abandon the district in which they had been working for some years, they expressed an earnest desire to see that mission still carried on, and intimated their readiness to place themselves under the supervision of the congregation which should

Yours faithfully

John Watson.

assume the direction of it. Mr. Watson lost
no time in communicating, through Dr. Miller,
the substance of this interview to his own
Session, who, appreciating the significance and
the delicacy of the position, requested both
ministers to meet with the Rev. James
Nicoll, of St. Stephen's, so as to obtain full
information on the matter in all its bearings.
In February they were able to report that
they had called upon Mr. Nicoll, who explained that his congregation had not seen its
way to continue operations at Springbank,
chiefly on account of the comparative want of
success in the endeavour to form an adult
congregation which might speedily be recognized as a sanctioned charge. He at the
same time bore willing testimony to the zeal
and success of the Sabbath School workers
among the children in that locality. Mr.
Watson further stated that after careful consideration, he had foreseen the impropriety, in
present circumstances, of entertaining these
proposals, unless, in some way, the Deacons'
Court could be relieved of all difficulty as to
expense in carrying on the new work. On
the strength of this conviction, he had, how-

ever, approached several members of the congregation, with the result that sufficient means had been already secured to meet half of the estimated expenditure for two years, while he expected farther promises of help within a few days.

A formal application, signed by thirty-three workers at Springbank, was then read, requesting the Session to take them and their work under congregational superintendence. The proposals, as now before the Session, were favourably entertained, and the whole question was referred to the Deacons' Court. When that Court met, Dr. Miller laid all the facts before it, and the following minute of the proceedings states the attitude ultimately assumed :

"After very serious and prolonged deliberation, the Court felt that it could not dutifully ignore this application ; and seeing that financial difficulties had been obviated without laying on the Court responsibilities which it could not undertake in present circumstances ; and seeing also that the work in Springbank can be carried on by the applicants without detriment to our own Mission work in Anderston : the Court, therefore, expresses its cordial sympathy with the proposed movement, and thinks that it ought to be carried out experimentally for at least one year, in the hope and with the prayer that the work of the Lord may be thereby promoted among a spiritually necessitous population."

Mr. Watson next communicated with the Rev. D. L. Kilpatrick, of North Woodside Free Church, as the minister nearest to the new district, and at once received from him expressions of satisfaction at the arrangements come to, and of his readiness to do all that lay in his power to forward the success of the undertaking.

Such was the manner in which Springbank Mission became grafted on the life of St. Matthew's, yet so interesting is the story of its own origin five years earlier, as we have heard it fervidly described by one of the chief movers in the matter, that we must spare a paragraph to give some account of this also.

Its genesis really dates from what is still spoken of as the "hundred and one night," and occurred on this wise. In the spring of 1874 a great wave of spiritual blessing followed in the wake of Mr. Moody's preaching. On one particular evening it seemed to reach high water mark. Overflowing meetings were being held in various parts of the city, at which Dr. Cairns of Berwick and Dr. Wilson of the Barclay Church were principal speakers. Curiously enough our present pastor, Dr. Stalker, happened to be an interested spectator. He was then finishing his course at the New College, and, along with Henry Drummond, came through as a deputation from the Edinburgh students. It was as late as ten o'clock when Mr. Moody, accompanied by these friends and other ministers, entered the meeting convened in Ewing Place Church and composed entirely of young men. The presence of God's Spirit was manifest from the first, and was felt by all. The meeting was prolonged till midnight, and ere it closed one hundred and one persons testified to their acceptance of the Saviour. That they had also been apprehended of Christ Jesus is evidenced by the consistent life and conversation of many to-day. It so happened that several of these were connected with Free St. Stephen's Church, and how to find scope for their freshly awakened zeal became a problem for its office-bearers. It was generally admitted that part of the north-west district was then comparatively neglected, and, accordingly, both Session and Deacons' Court were approached in the hope that mission work might be undertaken in that quarter. A formidable obstacle, however, stood in the way. There still remained a debt of £1500 on their church, and it was felt that further financial responsibility could not be incurred. At this juncture one of the elders (now a member of our own Session) generously volunteered to extinguish the liability; and so the way was cleared for the founding of Springbank Mission.

Premises were quickly secured, and it was decided to begin with a forenoon Foundry Boys' Meeting, a Sabbath School, and an evening service for adults. The question remained as to who should conduct these different enterprises, and the intending workers rightly felt that much depended upon this. They, therefore, made the matter a subject of earnest prayer in the first instance, and then resolved, *first*, that no one should be appointed to any post except by a unanimous vote; and, *secondly*, that no one thus chosen should refuse to act. In this way it came about that Mr. Robert Russell, our present elder, was elected chairman of the Foundry Boys' Meeting, and Mr. P. M'B. Stewart, now the devoted missionary of Cowcaddens Church, was elected superintendent of the Sabbath School; the evening meeting being left open for further arrangement.

Numbers of children were soon gathered in, and a work of grace followed. Within a short period seventy-five young people were noted, not merely as making some profession, but as having given evidence of a changed heart. Mr. Stewart, who has followed up these cases with peculiar interest, delights to bear testimony that in no single case have his hopes been disappointed.

After a few years, as we have said, financial and other considerations led the office-bearers of St. Stephen's to relinquish the work. Their decision was arrived at somewhat unexpectedly, and at first the workers were sorely perplexed. It occurred to one of them, however, on his way home from the meeting where the resolve was taken, to call upon Mr. Watson, to whom he was an entire stranger, and this he did, on his own responsibility, that very night. Ringing the bell at 42 Windsor Terrace with some trepidation, he found himself received with the utmost sympathy and consideration. Having listened to his tale, Mr. Watson encouraged him to believe that he had been rightly directed thither, and, before parting, knelt with him in prayer for further guidance. The various steps resulting from this interview have been already narrated.

Before passing from this subject it is worthy of note that, while without the hearty co-operation of St. Matthew's at this crisis, the Springbank Mission could not have been effectively carried on or developed, yet the new blood, then introduced, was of even greater value to St. Matthew's itself. Not only did it supply the most active agents at the Mission for more than a decade, but it has given to the congregation some of its most useful elders and deacons, including a General Treasurer, a Sustentation Fund Treasurer, a Foreign Mission Treasurer, and a Mission Convener.

In the Deacons' Court a full share of attention continued to be given to the Sustentation and Foreign Mission Funds, to Psalmody, and to the Day School at Anderston. It would appear that the last of these had not of late been producing quite such good results as formerly in the senior department. In the course of 1879, however, Mr. John W. J. Watt, then a teacher in the Normal Seminary, was appointed headmaster, and it is pleasing to read in next year's report of the Government Inspector : "This school, under the present teacher, shows a very gratifying rise in efficiency since last year."

Up to this time there had evidently existed some curious formalities as to the proper mode of ushering into church even regular worshippers, for in 1879, a special instruction to a new door-keeper is "that it is unnecessary to conduct to their seats, on Sabbaths, any but strangers who may inquire for a vacant seat."

In 1880 a proposal was broached to get rid of the remaining debt on the church, amounting to fully £1000, but before the matter could be dealt with, the distressing information reached the office-bearers that the junior pastor was about to receive a call from Liverpool.

On the 4th of August the Presbytery met to consider and decide the question of Mr. Watson's translation. There appeared for the Session, Messrs. G. M. Grierson, James M'Michael and Thomas Wharrie ; for the Deacons' Court, Messrs. M'Kill, Peter M'Kichan and William

Miller ; and for the congregation, Messrs. W.
R. Currie, John Kirsop, William Miller, John
C. Reid and Laurence Robertson. The
reasons set forth for the translation were
mainly that a church had just been erected
in the rising suburb of Sefton Park at a cost
of £8000, and that, with a minister of Mr.
Watson's gifts, there was every prospect of
forming a large and influential Presbyterian
congregation in an important English centre.
The call was signed by 70 members and 109
adherents, among whom, it was incidentally
mentioned, were two ministers' sons. These
statements were well met by a reference to
the admirable position of St. Matthew's Church,
the large membership, the existing harmony,
the happy prospects of the congregation with
a continuance of the present pastorate, and
the fact that in its Session alone there were
five sons of the manse!

When Mr. Watson was called upon, he said
that the matter had caused him much anxious
and painful consideration, and that he had
endeavoured to give conscientious attention
to the pleadings on both sides. He felt
impressed by the claims of English Presby-

terianism, the special nature of the sphere offered, the noble efforts already made in Sefton Park, and the difficulty which that congregation might experience in obtaining a suitable minister within their own small communion. On the other hand, there could not but weigh with him the shortness of his ministry in St. Matthew's, the measure of success which, by God's blessing, had attended it, the cordial relations subsisting between himself and his beloved father, Dr. Miller, and the good feeling of office-bearers and people, among whom were some of the most loyal adherents possessed by the Free Church. On the ground of attachment to Dr. Miller alone, he had frequently inclined to remain where he was, though he also felt that too much weight ought not to be given to a purely personal consideration. On the whole, he had come to the conclusion that he ought to accept the Liverpool call, not as to an easier or more certain position, but as to an opportunity for great work, and from a desire to resume the undivided charge of a congregation. His conviction was that the work put before him on leaving Logiealmond—that of reorganizing a congregation which had passed through a severe trial—had been largely accomplished, and that St. Matthew's might now obtain a worthier man.

In view of this frank and explicit statement, the Presbytery had no alternative but to acquiesce in Mr. Watson's removal, rejoicing at the same time that St. Matthew's found itself in such a strong and united position.

On Sabbath, 26th September, a farewell sermon was preached by Mr. Watson, and at the first meeting of Session thereafter the court recorded

"their sorrow at his translation from this congregation, to which he had so fully commended himself by an earnest and able pastorate of three years. They have ever been appreciative of his talents in the pulpit, his devotedness to all pastoral work, the amiability of his intercourse, and the hearty geniality of his whole deportment among them. They trust he will be as highly esteemed in his new sphere, that his days of active labour may be many, and that he may have much comfort and a goodly harvest of souls as the fruit of his ministry in the congregation of which he is now sole pastor. And while their prayers for these blessings follow him, they also seek to be much in prayer that the Lord of the vineyard will, in His good pleasure, provide a suitable successor for him in St. Matthew's, who shall be greatly owned of God to feed our people with the Bread and Water of life."

Mr. Watson carried with him to Liverpool a pledge which must ever remind him of St. Matthew's, for while in Glasgow he married Jane, daughter of the late Mr. Francis J. Ferguson, to whom reference has already been made in this narrative as one of the most useful elders of the congregation.   Since going south, he has received the degree of D.D. from St. Andrews University, and " Dr. Watson of Liverpool" has become his familiar designation.

It would be an impertinence at this time of day to add almost a word about one who has in recent years become so widely known under the name of Ian Maclaren. The volume which first brought him into fame, entitled *Beside the Bonnie Brier Bush*, abounds in accurate and appreciative delineations of homely religious character as exhibited in our Scottish Midlands, and its more pathetic passages cannot be read in any company capable of understanding their inwardness, without a tremor in the voice, or, it may be, a tear in the eye.

The book has enjoyed a quite phenomenal circulation, not only in our own country, but also in America, while others of Dr. Watson's works come little behind it in this respect. The great popularity thus acquired on the other side of the Atlantic led to his being asked a year or two later to deliver a course of lectures at Yale University, and these have since been published under the title of *The Cure of Souls*. So fertile has been his faculty of authorship, that within the past five years no fewer than seven considerable volumes have issued from his pen. Among these may be mentioned *The Mind of the Master*, *The Potter's Wheel*, and *The Upper Room*, the last of which is a particularly beautiful and suggestive devotional study.

Dr. Watson is convener of the College Committee of the Presbyterian Church of England, and is already spoken of as a future Moderator of its Synod. It need hardly be added that it is a pleasure to many old friends, when at some anniversary of Church or Mission, his voice is still occasionally heard from the pulpit of St. Matthew's.

H

VII
Mr. Salmond's Ministry
1881 86

"And of Zion it shall be said, This and that man was born in her: and the Highest Himself shall establish her."

PSALM lxxxvii. 5.

Mr. Salmond's Ministry
1881-86

THE congregation of St. Matthew's, having been thus unexpectedly deprived of their junior pastor, at once proceeded to look round about for that worthy successor to whom Mr. Watson had pointed them. Nor did hearty unanimity fail them in the quest. Within three months from the date of the vacancy, they, with one consent, made choice of the Rev. Chas. A. Salmond, M.A., who had been, for a year or two, settled at Cults in Aberdeenshire. His record was that of an Edinburgh student of much promise, who had enjoyed the additional advantage of a session at Princeton, U.S., under Drs. Chas. and A. A. Hodge. The promptitude of the selection gave unfeigned delight to Dr. Miller, and was also a happy augury for the future.

The following commissioners prosecuted the call ; from the Session, Messrs. Grierson, M'Michael and Wharrie ; from the Deacons' Court, Messrs. Currie and M'Kichan; and from the congregation, Messrs. Fulton and Kirsop; along with the Rev. Dr. Adam as representing the Presbytery. A telegram from Aberdeen, read at the prayer-meeting on 17th February, 1881, brought the discouraging information that the Presbytery had refused to translate. Next day Dr. Miller wrote : " Dear Mr. Salmond,— The telegram which I received yesterday at 3.20 p.m. smote me down very much ; and when the news reached the congregation in the evening, every one was bitterly grieved and disappointed. I am glad to find to-day that an appeal was taken to the Synod, and I may say to you at once that the St. Matthew's people will not fall from that appeal, but will prosecute it, in the earnest hope that we may yet succeed in securing you as co-pastor. O how gladly would we all hail such a consummation!" When the Synod met on 12th April, it sent Mr. Salmond to Glasgow.

Yours very truly,
Charles A. Salmond

On Friday, 13th May, a social meeting to welcome the new colleague was held in the Queen's Rooms, at which, as we have seen, Dr. Miller was present, meeting his people there for the last time. On Sabbath the 15th, Mr. Salmond was introduced by his old professor, Dr. George Smeaton.

If the death of Dr. Samuel Miller, within two months of this auspicious settlement, was a painful shock to his attached congregation, the blow fell with double weight upon his newly-inducted colleague. In concluding his first sermon after the funeral, Mr. Salmond said : "I shall not intrude upon you to-day my own personal anxieties, for I need not lay claim in words to your sympathy and forbearance in going forward to the enhanced responsibilities that lie before me. It is to me a solemn reflection that Dr. Miller's last public act was to bid me welcome to the work of the Lord among you. Pray for me, that I may be worthy of the sacred trust!" Thus pathetically did the new ministry open in tears, and so it was with sorrowful, yet courageous hearts that minister and people together went forward towards the solution of various problems which already waited attention.

The first of these was how to deal with the ancient balance of debt, amounting to £1034, which still rested upon the church fabric. A vigorous effort was therefore inaugurated to extinguish this obligation, and it was at the same time proposed to place in the vestibule of Free St. Matthew's a marble bust of its first minister. " This," as the office-bearers put it to the congregation, "would form a two-fold opportunity which could not recur, of at once honouring the memory of the pastor deceased, and of heartening, in present and future effort, him whom God had placed in his room." In February, 1882, it was announced that the double scheme had been completely successful, and that the modelling of a medallion bust had been entrusted to Mr. Mossman, sculptor. The result may be seen in that speaking likeness which meets every eye on entering the church.

It soon came to be felt that the relation of St. Matthew's to mission work in Anderston had drifted into a somewhat anomalous position. Cranstonhill Church had for a number of years

been the recognized outcome of early labours
there, yet we still continued our Sabbath
school, kitchen meetings, and Bible woman
in complete, though by no means unfriendly,
independence of it. While this could never
have been regarded as either a desirable
or permanent arrangement, attention was
pointedly called to the matter on the formation of the Glasgow Home Mission Union,
which had for its objects the suppression of
overlapping and the allocation of a definite
district to each co-operating congregation.
In these circumstances it was dutifully agreed
by Cransfonhill and ourselves to approach,
first of all, our own Presbytery for advice.
After hearing parties at length, the Presbytery recommended that the Anderston district
should henceforth belong exclusively to Cranstonhill, St. Matthew's being encouraged to
fulfil its maternal instincts by a contribution of £25 for three years or so, to help in
the efficient carrying on of aggressive work
round that church.

The various agencies with which St. Matthew's had for forty years been identified
were accordingly withdrawn, or rather trans-

ferred. In March, 1884, a leaflet was issued,
from which we cull the following sentences:

"In reluctantly giving up Sabbath School work, so
long carried on in Anderston, we, the superintendents
and teachers, desire affectionately to express the hope
that the parents of our scholars will make sure that their
children immediately connect themselves with some other
evangelical school in the district. We are glad to announce that arrangements have been made whereby all
our scholars will be heartily welcomed at Cranstonhill
Free Church school, and we recommend that this be
freely taken advantage of. We intend to introduce them
personally to the new school, and our hearts' desire and
prayer for each and all is that they may grow up into
Christ in all things.

In name of the Sabbath School Teachers,

G. E. PHILIP and J. W. J. WATT,

Joint Superintendents."

A neatly lithographed card was at the same
time presented to every child, certifying that
he or she was a member of Free St. Matthew's
school at the date of its removal from the
district. After assembling one evening for
the last time in the old building, a procession
of teachers and scholars wended its way across
Main Street to Cranstonhill Church, where
they had a cordial reception from the Rev.
Mr. Linn and his staff of teachers, a few of
our own continuing their help for some time

until the children got accustomed to their new surroundings.

To many of the senior workers in Anderston the closing of their familiar school-house, with all its memories, was a sore trial; yet it had become abundantly evident that the guiding pillar was leading elsewhere. In due time the premises, which had been latterly rented to the School Board, were sold, and by the severance of this last link with the district, we found ourselves free to concentrate every resource on the rapidly developing field at Springbank. The Session, in their annual report, say that "they have sympathized to the full with the feelings of those whose long attachment to Anderston district has made it a real trial to leave it; and they have done their utmost to secure that the interests of that district may not suffer. They consider that the spirit shown by the body of teachers and other workers in connection with this matter has been truly admirable." Amongst these, few had been more indefatigable than Messrs. James Imrie, James Glass and William Kirkland, all of whom are represented in the congregation to-day. We are also glad to have still in our midst the family of Mr. John Wilson, the first and peculiarly devoted mission convener, as well as Mr. James Miller, a later convener of Dr. Miller's days.

While, for the sake of continuity, we have brought down the history of the Anderston Mission to its close in 1884, it is now necessary to go back a year or two in order to keep in hand the threads of interest which were rapidly attaching us to Springbank. It will be remembered that work in the north-west district had in Mr. Watson's time been only tentatively undertaken for a couple of years or so. In December, 1881, however, Mr. Pratt formally raised the whole question of its future, both in Session and Deacons' Court, with the result that it was definitely agreed " to unite the new mission, with all its concerns and interests, to that of Anderston." Again, two years later, the Session "learned with satisfaction that the joint committee of the different churches have assigned to St. Matthew's a free field in the district where we have been already working." This, of course, refers to the admirably conceived sub-division of the city by the Home Mission

Union, whose functions we have already described.

The portion for which we thus became responsible consisted of a triangular district, bounded by Well Road, Garscube Road, and New City Road. The premises hitherto rented above a large spirit shop at the junction of Garscube and New City Roads were also triangular in form. Many will remember the little room snipped off the apex, where the senior class of boys was cooped up amid the banners and boxes of a Good Templar lodge, whose grand masters were in possession on certain evenings of the week. Then there was the unpromising room at the farther end, deducted from the Bible woman's house, where Mrs. Black and Miss Macfadzean found cramped accommodation for a numerous following of senior girls, with the rotunda upstairs, where the grown-up lads held high revel when not under the spell of their regular teacher.

To remedy this state of things, Mr. Pratt, in April, 1884, brought before the Session the necessity of providing more suitable premises. The great difficulty was where to find these, and, as temporary expedients, the infant

class was taken at an earlier hour than the
rest of the school, while an empty shop was
secured for certain of the other meetings.
By December, however, the Deacons' Court
saw their way to purchase a plot of ground
in Doncaster Street at 20s. per square yard,
in anticipation of an early sale of the Anderston property.   Plans having been prepared
by Mr. Wharrie, and estimates accepted, a
memorial stone was laid on 8th August, 1885,
by Mr. Salmond, who at the same time
placed in the cavity a narrative of the Mission, a congregational manual, and other
items.   He subsequently addressed those present on the "Stone of Help," and the "Stone
of Watching," being followed by Mr. Russell,
who spoke of the "Retrospect and Prospect."
"Thereafter," we read, "the throng dispersed,
feeling that it was a memorable day alike
for the congregation of St. Matthew's and
for the district of Springbank."

On Friday, 26th March, 1886, our model
mission premises, as we fondly regarded them,
were formally opened in presence of a large
gathering, appropriate addresses being delivered by Mr. Salmond, Dr. Andrew A. Bonar,

Dr. Dalzell of the Gordon Mission, Professor Drummond, Mr. Wharrie, and Mr. R. E. Aitken, congregational treasurer. A full description of the buildings appeared in the *Herald* next day, but as most of us are a good deal more familiar with them than the reporter, we refrain from burdening our narrative with his account.

In the same month Miss Campbell, whose name has since become a household word in every home, was appointed Bible woman. In October the Lord's Supper was dispensed for the first time, under authority of the Presbytery, when twenty-nine persons, chiefly from among the lapsed, were admitted to membership, as a nucleus round which it was hoped to gather others. It only remains to add that the sum of £1200, required beyond the price realised by the sale of the Anderston schoolhouse, was readily subscribed.

As in Dr. Miller's ministry, so now, the Musical Association and Psalmody Committee from time to time asserted themselves as factors that had to be reckoned with. In 1883 they jointly petitioned the session to sanction the practice of standing during praise, "having long felt that the present arrangement (of sitting) is unsatisfactory and militates against a worthy expression of heart-felt praise." In acceding to this suggestion the cautious Session "recommended the petitioners and the congregation generally to maintain the standing posture during prayer also, and asked the moderator so to arrange the reading of Scripture as to make standing at both no real inconvenience, except to the aged and infirm, who cannot be expected to stand at either." It may seem strange that no explanation was offered as to why the recommendation did not also include standing during the reading of God's word, for which there would seem to be at least equal authority (Neh. viii. 5, etc.).

In 1884, the Psalmody Committee further asked the sanction of the Court to "the use of the *Free Church Hymnal* in conjunction with the Psalms in the ordinary worship of the congregation." Although there was found to be little difference of opinion on the ground of principle, considerable doubt existed as to the ripeness of the congregation for the change proposed. It was, however, decided by a majority "that the adoption of the *Free*

Church Hymnal will enable us, without de-
priving the Psalms of their leading place in
the praise of God, to have the occasional benefit
of well approved hymns, which express in
gospel language ideas and aspects of truth
revealed with peculiar clearness in New Testament times. The Session cherish the confident expectation that this addition to our
service of praise will be received with satisfaction by the congregation generally, and at
least acquiesced in cheerfully by any of our
members who may not yet for themselves
be prepared to welcome it." It was a matter
of sincere regret, at the time, that several of
our attached people, including one elder and
other earnest workers, felt constrained to leave
St. Matthew's when this decision was intimated;
though it is pleasing also to record that some
of these soon saw their way to rejoin us.

While touching on psalmody, we must not
omit to mention that, in the end of 1881, the
congregation had been fortunate in securing
the services of Mr. W. H. Murray as praise
leader, a choice which has proved of incal-
culable benefit to all the interests concerned.
For seventeen years he has successfully sought

to infuse the devotional spirit of praise among old and young, and his illustrated lectures on Music and Song, delivered at joint meetings of the Young Men's and Young Women's Unions, have been looked forward to as annual treats.

In 1883 it was resolved to hold a summer communion for the benefit of such as might be still in town, and the attendance proved so considerable, that the practice has never since been departed from. In October, 1884, the method of simultaneous communion was adopted, and has been found greatly to promote quiet and decorum.

In the winters of 1882-83, and 1884-85, Mr. Salmond held a series of most successful family gatherings. All the members and adherents in two or three contiguous districts met with their elders, deacons, and minister in the Deacons' Court Room, tastefully arranged for the occasion. The programme was—"half an hour for tea, three quarters of an hour for addresses, three quarters of an hour for conversation, closing with family worship before ten o'clock." It was at one of these that "Gilbert" (Wilson), who was about to remove to a distance, was presented with a marble time-piece as a token of regard. He humorously described himself as "the oldest member of the firm," having been one of the original 44 who in the year '44 gathered round Dr. Miller, from the first day of whose ministry till now he had acted as doorkeeper.

Special attention was paid during these years to the systematic visitation of the three Sabbath schools by elders in rotation, and their interesting monthly reports were amongst the stated items of Session business. In 1883 we find there were 200 young men and women in the minister's Bible class, besides 580 children on the rolls of the various schools. The Savings-banks were particularly flourishing institutions, no fewer than 7318 separate transactions being reported from Anderston, and 2271 from Spring-bank in a single year. The following letter, which we print exactly as received by the Anderston superintendent, may be taken as an illustration of the power of conscience to quicken seed sown by a possibly disheartened teacher :

"To the head teacher of Free st Matthew's school.

"Dear Sir,—I send you three shillings in postage stamps

for the Misshinary box. some years agoe I attended st
matthews sabath school the csholars cllecting for a new
missinary ship and I also and I kept back part of the money
I think it was about nine pence i sthank god he did not
strike me doune dead Like Annis and sappria I have been
living without god in the world all my life and God has
arrasted me in my doward course. O that God would have
marce one my soule. pray to God to have marce on me.
the other 2/ and three pence I pray that may be the
means helping the good work. I conclude

I am a hardened sinner."

A friendly rivalry seems to have existed
between the treasurers of the Sustentation and
Foreign Mission Funds, for while in July, 1882,
it is pointed out by Mr. Currie, that, with £785
as our annual contribution to the Sustentation
Fund, we stood *fourth* in the Presbytery and
eleventh in the Church, Mr. M'Kichan next
month calls attention to the other fact that,
with £127 to Foreign Missions, we only stood
sixth in the Presbytery and *fifteenth* in the
Church. An effort to place this latter fund
in a worthier position followed, and, in 1884,
we find that the situation is reversed. With
£758 for the Sustentation Fund we were then
fifth in the Presbytery and *thirteenth* in the
Church, while, with £180 for Foreign Missions,
we were *third* in the Presbytery and *sixth* in

the Church. It will, of course, be understood that this last figure refers to the amount remitted to the central fund only, and does not include auxiliary efforts on behalf of female education in India and Africa, China Mission, or other subsidiary schemes. It may be mentioned, for instance, that when, in 1886, Mr. Philip, who had assumed the treasurership, issued a first appeal on behalf of Livingstonia, £30 was at once contributed for this object alone.

A congregational supplement to the *Free Church Monthly* was added in 1882, and the *Record Cover* has since become an indispensable medium for conveying information about the varied organizations and interests of St. Matthew's. Ably edited from the first, it is now in the hands of an experienced journalist, and promises to make the work of a future historian easy indeed, if not entirely superfluous.

In November, 1883, Mr. Salmond married Margaret H. Hammersley, daughter of the Rev. Thomas Johnston of Killarney. The welcome accorded to the young bride represented much kindly feeling, and Mrs. Salmond

soon took a warm place in the affections of
the people. She will be specially remembered
as first president of the newly formed Young
Women's Union.

In January, 1886, Mr. John Macfarlane,
elder, was removed by death, "ever conspicuous for his humble Christian character
and example"; and, towards the end of the
same year, Dr. Ebenezer Watson also, remarkable for "the long and consistent discharge of duty alike as an eminent member
of his profession, and as an office-bearer in
this congregation." Nor must we forget to
mention two notable lady members who passed
away in the autumn of 1883. Miss Paterson,
who had been Bible woman in Anderston for
the long period of twenty-three years, was
greatly beloved in the district where she
laboured so devotedly, and highly esteemed
by the Ladies' Association, who best knew
her worth. Miss Eliza Fletcher—a biography
of whom, by Mr. Salmond, had an ex-
tensive sale—was a magnetic force of no
ordinary attractiveness amongst those for
whom she laboured. With untiring zeal she
conducted large classes of young women in

various parts of the city, and her "praise was in all the churches." Dr. Watson of Sefton Park, writing at the time of her death, said, " She impressed me as a woman of passionate nature, consecrated to Christ—a true type of the Christian enthusiast dashed with real genius."

In November, 1886, a call to Mr. Salmond from the Free West Church, Rothesay, as colleague and successor to the venerable Dr. Elder, was initiated. Whenever this became known the elders convened, and hastened to assure their minister of the high satisfaction it would afford them to learn that he had resolved to remain in Free St. Matthew's. On 6th December, however, Mr. Salmond intimated to his Session that, after full consideration, he felt he ought to go. When this disappointing information reached the Deacons' Court, they immediately drew up for presentation an appreciative letter, which was signed by every one of the twenty-one deacons.

At the Presbytery, which met on the 13th, Messrs. Thomas Wharrie and G. E. Philip represented the Session, and while offering no opposition in view of Mr. Salmond's declared mind, they bore willing testimony to the zeal, energy and success of the ministry about to close, and specially to the unremitting attention bestowed upon the poor, the lonely, and the sick. He had put the congregation in thorough working order, and whoever might fill his place would find it an easier matter to carry on the work. Mr. Salmond, in stating his own clear judgment, referred to the painful trial so unexpectedly encountered at the beginning of his pastorate, through the death of Dr. Miller, the five and a half busy, happy and not unfruitful years which followed, the loyal support of his office-bearers during a transition stage of congregational history, the new organizations and needful modifications of old arrangements which had been carried through, and the life-long inspiration derived from contact with Christian brethren in this great city. On the motion of Dr. Adam, the translation was agreed to.

In thus losing Mr. Salmond, the congregation of St. Matthew's were conscious of parting with one whose preaching had been acceptable and profitable, and who was ever willing to spend and be spent in their service. The

Deacons' Court could not but remember his strenuous efforts in connection with the handsome Mission Halls at Springbank, which remain as a fitting memorial of his pastorate. The Session could also point to a membership increased by 150, no fewer than 229 having been admitted for the first time; and they only regretted that he was leaving at a time when he had hardly seen the fruit of much good seed carefully sown.

Though a change to some less exacting sphere was probably desirable just then in the interest of Mr. Salmond's own health, after the exceptional strain through which he had passed, it could scarcely be expected that he would long remain "a country brother." In three years he was once more translated, and has since been instrumental in building up an important congregation at South Morningside, Edinburgh. He is the author of *Princetoniana*, a collection of interesting reminiscences of the eminent professors under whom he studied in America; of *For Days of Youth*, being Text and Talk for every day; and of Bible Class Primers on *The Christian Passover* and *The Sabbath*.

VIII

Dr. Stalker's Ministry
1887-98

" Look upon Zion, the city of our solemnities : thine eyes shall see Jerusalem a quiet habitation. . . . There the glorious Lord will be unto us a place of broad rivers and streams."

ISAIAH xxxiii. 20, 21.

Dr. Stalker's Ministry
1887-98

W E may now be said to have reached the period of modern history, in the making of which many of those now with us have had some share.

When, on previous occasions, St. Matthew's was in quest of a minister, he was wanted as colleague to Dr. Miller, who, all the while, continued to act as moderator of Session. Now, for the first time, we were without a head, and were, therefore, well pleased when the Presbytery gave us the Rev. Andrew Melville of St. Enoch's as interim-moderator. Mr. Salmond's induction at Rothesay having been postponed till 1st February, 1887, it was only after that date that we were in a position to take formal steps towards securing a successor. The interval was not, however, without its advantages. We became conscious that, with unity amongst ourselves, we might expect to obtain one of the very best ministers the Church could supply, and a frank interchange of ideas showed that such unity was attainable. Mr. M'Michael, senior elder, was chosen chairman of the large selection committee, and, under his prudent guidance, matters were not long in ripening. At a congregational meeting held on the last day of February, it was resolved to give a hearty call to the Rev. James Stalker, M.A., of Kirkcaldy.

Mr. Stalker had become widely known as the author of two admirably concise and graphic hand-books on the *Life of Christ* and the *Life of St. Paul.* His college career had been full of distinction ; as assistant for a time to Dr. J. H. Wilson of the Barclay Church, Edinburgh, he enjoyed the advantage of invaluable early training ; while as minister of St. Brycedale for twelve years, he had given proof of his ministry in the building up of a congregation eight or nine hundred strong, which had just crowned his labours by rearing a church edifice of noble proportions. He had, a few years before, married Charlotte, daughter of Francis Brown Douglas, Esq., a former Lord Provost of the city of Edinburgh, whose family has always been closely identified with the Free Church.

Presbyterial machinery makes haste slowly, but on 27th April, the Kirkcaldy Presbytery at last met to receive our commissioners. These were Rev. Dr. Adam and Rev. W. R. Taylor from the Presbytery; Messrs. James M'Michael, G. E. Philip and Robert Russell from the Session; Mr. Wm. Black from the Deacons' Court; and Mr. John Boag from the congregation.

Mr. Ross Taylor, in opening the case for St. Matthew's, referred to the admirably mixed character of the congregation, its central position in Glasgow, and its proximity to the haunts of students and young men. Mr. Philip emphasized the enthusiasm of the call, which bore 640 signatures, the honourable history and present activity of the congregation, together with the opportunity its pulpit presented for extended influence in the metropolis of the west. He was confident that, with a wise head to guide, a warm heart to encourage, and good preaching to provide nutriment, St. Matthew's would, by the blessing of God, continue to flourish. Mr. Russell followed with a lucid description of the various agencies at work in the mission district, and dwelt on the inspiration to be derived from contact with the manifold activities of a great city. Mr. Boag having added a word, ex-Provost Swan intimated that the St. Brycedale people had sorrowfully resolved to place no obstacle in Mr. Stalker's way, should he see it to be his duty to leave them at this time.

Mr. Stalker, when called upon, said that the appeal, conveyed through St. Matthew's congregation, had grown more distinct and impressive, till he had been forced to recognize in it the voice of God. He had decided to join himself to those who were seeking to leaven Glasgow with the gospel of Christ. He sought not rest, but a fuller life, and the real fascination of the call lay in the stimulus which he anticipated from the religious enterprise of that city. Whatever the future might bring, however, the twelve years spent in

Kirkcaldy would always appear in retrospect a sunny portion of his journey through life.

On the motion of the Rev. Norman Walker of Dysart, seconded by the Rev. P. M'Ainsh of Lochgelly, the translation was agreed to, and our commissioners, after being hospitably entertained by Mr. Swan, returned home grateful to God for the happy issue of their errand to the east.

On the 17th May Mr. Stalker was inducted to the charge of Free St. Matthew's, the Rev. John Scott of the West Church presiding. A conversazione was held in the evening, when members of the congregation had an opportunity of individually welcoming the new minister. Among the speakers were Revs. C. A. Salmond, G. A. Smith and Norman Walker, Professor Drummond and ex-Provost Swan. Mr. Laurence Robertson presented Mr. Stalker with gown, Bible, Psalm and Hymn Book, while Mr. M'Michael handed a suitable acknowledgment to the interim-moderator. On Sabbath 22nd, Mr. Stalker was introduced by the Rev. Dr. J. H. Wilson, and in the afternoon preached himself, to an overflowing audience, on "Motives for the

K

Christian Ministry," from 2 Cor. iv. 5 : " We preach not ourselves but Christ Jesus the Lord, and ourselves your servants for Jesus' sake"; the passion for self, for Christ, and for man. Thus auspiciously commenced the pastorate, which happily continues to the present time in unabated vigour and with growing appreciation.

Such epochs in a congregation's life are usually attended with unavoidable changes in the *personnel* of its working staff. Honoured office-bearers who have been induced to retain their posts, almost in spite of necessity, during an existing ministry, at length find it their duty to sever the well-loved connection. And so it happened that we were all at once called upon to bid farewell to Mr. G. M. Grierson, who had long done yeoman service in the department of finance ; to Mr. R. E. Aitken, general treasurer ; and to two other old and trusted elders, all on account of excessive distance from church. Mr. Wharrie also, for the same reason, intimated that he would no longer be able to discharge the duties of Session-clerk, though willing to give whatever help he could as an elder without a district.

In accepting Mr. Wharrie's resignation, the
Session resolved to minute "their high appreciation of the long and faithful services he has
rendered in the eleven years during which
he has adorned the office of Session-clerk.
Called to the post at a difficult period in the
history of the congregation, his tact has been
conspicuously exercised in the election of no
fewer than three successive ministers, while
his manifold labours, wise counsels, and un-
failing courtesy have ever deeply impressed
his brethren. In now acceding to his request
to be relieved of his more onerous duties, their
earnest desire is that he may be long spared
for much usefulness in the Church, and that,
in the future as in the past, they may frequently benefit by his genial presence and
ripe experience." Mr. George E. Philip was
appointed in his room.

In minuting the acceptance of Mr. Aitken's
resignation, the Deacons' Court "particularly
recognized his services (along with those of
Mr. M'Michael) in connection with the clear-
ing of the debt at Springbank, and with the
sale of the Anderston property." Mr. William
Black was appointed his successor.

To the delight of all, the other two brethren soon found that their affection for St. Matthew's so greatly exceeded the distance they had to travel, that at a special congregational meeting they were heartily welcomed back to office within six months of demitting it, and are still in active service.

With nets thus mended, and the church itself freshly decorated, the winter's work was entered upon with high hope and courage. Large accessions of members immediately began to flow in, and have continued so to do, till at the present moment our membership is almost doubled. This is the more gratifying when we remember that, in a central city congregation like our own, it requires as many as 110 additions annually, if numbers are even to be maintained.

In order the better to supervise this ever-increasing congregation, frequent elections of elders and deacons have become necessary, no fewer than five ordinations to each office having taken place during the past eleven years, adding in all about ninety members to the roll of Deacons' Court. Supplementary lists of adherents, and of children were early

devised by Mr. David MacLean, who has since
taken infinite pains in keeping them up to
date. In addition to this, a standing Strangers'
Committee was appointed with the double object
of giving a hearty welcome to · new-comers,
whether casual or permanent, and of intro-
ducing them to church fellowship and work.
Its services have been warmly appreciated by
many, and its occasional reunions have well
answered the purpose for which they were
intended.

Difficulty was by-and-by felt by the seat-
letting committee in satisfying the requirements
of all who applied for sittings, and additional
discretionary power had to be granted them,
by way of increasing somewhat the total
number available, and especially of facilitating
provision for families and *bonâ fide* members.
The tact displayed by successive conveners
has ever proved equal to the occasion, and
nearly all have been sooner or later accommodated without friction.

As the natural result of all this, congregational income rose rapidly until we were
in the happy position of being able to dispense
entirely with special and spasmodic efforts.

An analysis of an ordinary church-door collection, casually made in 1889, may not be without interest, as giving some idea of the attendance at both diets of worship. The following are the number and value of coins put into the plate on 15th September:

FORENOON.		£	s.	d.		AFTERNOON.		£	s.	d.
92	- ½d.	0	3	10	112	- ½d.	0	4	8
444	- 1d.	1	17	0	452	- 1d.	1	17	8
49	- 3d.	0	12	3	40	- 3d.	0	10	0
71	- 6d.	1	15	6	38	- 6d.	0	19	0
14	- 1s.	0	14	0	13	- 1s.	0	13	0
3	- 2s.	0	6	0	1	- 2s.	0	2	0
673 Coins,	£5	8	7		656 Coins,	£4	6	4		

Total for day, £9 14s. 11d.

For the first six years, contributions to the Sustentation Fund also steadily increased, till they reached £917. They have since rather receded owing to the inevitable lapsing of certain considerable subscriptions, and their replacement by smaller ones. While some variation must be allowed for in a congregation composed like our own, it is quite felt that if the vital importance of this fund were gener-

or say £1000 at least, might be attained.
Nothing, certainly, has been wanting on the
part of the treasurers to ensure careful in-
gathering, and many contribute well up to
their ability, yet it is too patent that some
of our younger wage-earners are slow to begin,
and forgetful to revise their giving in this
particular direction. As Mr. Currie, in one of
his weighty *Record-cover* paragraphs remarks :
" If a member of the Free Church gives to
any religious or charitable object, surely it
ought to be first and most largely to the fund
which is the mainstay, if not the sole support,
of a large proportion of her ministers. That
their incomes are not too high will be seen
when it is stated that only four per cent. have
£500 a year and upwards, while 500 have
less than £200 a year." At the same time
it is a remarkable and creditable fact, that in
the 55 years since the Disruption, close upon
£55,000 has been remitted by St. Matthew's
to this fund.

With regard to the great work of Foreign
Missions, interest has certainly deepened. Not
only have contributions through the regular
Missionary Association steadily advanced, but

numerous auxiliary schemes have from time to time received warm support. In 1889, a commendable departure was made by Mr. Russell in the formation of a Juvenile Association, with periodically opened missionary boxes in the homes of its members. Thirteen of these were taken up during the first year, and the contents have gone to support a girl in training for mission work at the Madras Institution.

The appointment of Dr. Sandilands, one of our members, to Bhandara in the same year, was made the occasion of furnishing him with books and medical outfit to the value of £58, while a native assistant was also provided for a year or two thereafter.

When the Rev. Wm. Ewing, a former assistant, went to Tiberias a little later, a valuable library of research was gifted, chiefly by the Bible Class. In acknowledging its subsequent completion Mr. Ewing wrote:

"It is one of the best, if not the very best of its kind in the country. It comprises volumes on the geology of the Holy Land, its geography, history, antiquities, people, religion, manners and customs; also books of travel, ancient and modern. 'Memoirs' and 'Special Papers,' their large Survey map, and beautiful set of drawings illustrative of excavations in Jerusalem, have been added by officers of that Fund and others. The books are most comfortably housed in a handsome bookcase, also kindly provided by you. Over it in black ornamental letters on a white ground stands the legend 'Tiberias Mission Library, the gift of Free St. Matthew's, Glasgow.' It will be of great value for reference to travellers in Palestine."

A cot in the hospital there has also been maintained for many years by the Christian Endeavour Society at Springbank.

In 1893, the sum of £155 was contributed to the "Foreign Mission Jubilee Thank-offering," one donation being accompanied by this note : "A humble mite from two Disruption worthies, who, on the second Sabbath of July, 1843, sat at the communion in the green field." Waldensian Missions have been granted a subsidy of £20 for several years. China and Livingstonia have not been forgotten. Appeals from Armenia, Persia, India, Africa, Belgium, and Canada have also been responded to.

The most important effort in this department, however, has been that inaugurated by Mrs. Stalker and a committee of ladies in 1896, whereby it is intended to support a lady missionary of our own in India. A sale of work was held in the spring of 1897, which, with a few added subscriptions, realized sufficient to carry out this object for two years. Miss Annie Douglas, who used to be a member of St. Matthew's, and whose brother is also a missionary in India, has thus become our representative, and is settled at Jalna, the scene of Narayan Sheshadri's labours.

With Rev. John C. Gibson in Swatow and Rev. Andrew B. Nielson in Formosa; with Rev. Dr. M'Kichan in the College and Rev. Robert M. Gray in the church at Bombay; with Rev. Dr. Sandilands at Bhandara and his brother Dr. James at Santo, New Hebrides; with Rev. Donald Fraser at Livingstonia and Rev. C. W. Fleming in South Africa; with Rev. J. H. Maclean at Madras, the Rev. R. B. Douglas and his sister at Jalna, and Miss Gault at Benares; St. Matthew's can scarcely be other than a missionary congregation. Some of us also remember Alexander Menzies and Robert White, who, in recent years, laid down their lives in China and Africa; nor do we forget Rev. Walter G. Maclaren, who has long been settled at Bluff, New Zealand, or Rev. David Ross, who, having ministered for

SOME RECENT ASSISTANTS.

Rev. R. M. Gray, M.A. Bombay.	Rev. J. B. Johnstone, B.D. Falkirk.	Rev. William Hay, B.D. Ayr.
Rev. R. Scrymgeour, M.A. Jersey.	Rev. R. G. Philip, M.A. Glencairn.	Rev. C. W. Fleming, B.D. Inclive, S. Africa.
Rev. A. R. Gordon, M.A. Monikie.	Rev. David Young, M.A. Partick.	Rev. Hugh MacLauslin, Irvine.

some years in the beautiful parish of Crathie,
close to Balmoral, has now a flourishing charge
in Perth, Western Australia.

In the Home field the multiform operations
at Springbank have been carried on with increasing vigour and success. In the next
chapter we hope to say something of these
in detail, but may here mention that about
£200 per annum is expended on that district,
in addition to some £80 derived from invested
funds. The membership, which in 1887 was
forty, has now almost trebled. House-building
in the immediate neighbourhood of our premises
has taken rapid strides, whole streets of fully
occupied tenements now covering spaces which
but the other day appeared to be "no man's
land." In view of these and other circumstances which will be referred to, it seemed to
many as if matters were ripe for a forward
movement, and in January, 1897, Dr. Stalker
was able to make an important statement to
the congregation, from which we take the
following sentences :

"Our Mission sprang, I am told, out of the revival
movement associated with the name of Mr. Moody, which
swept over the city in 1874. It was at first connected

with St. Stephen's Church, but was subsequently transferred
to St. Matthew's; and very handsome and commodious
premises were erected for the prosecution of the work.
It has been a great blessing to the Springbank district,
and it has been a great blessing to this congregation.

"I am not sure whether those who started it at first
had any very clear views as to what it should ultimately
become. It was to be a centre of evangelistic effort—a
means of making known the Gospel—perhaps this was
all they were thinking of at first. But the best traditions
of such work in this city point in the direction of an effort
of the kind culminating in the founding of a new congregation; and it is several years since the Presbytery of the
bounds represented to our office-bearers the desirability
of keeping this in view. The call, however, to take any
new step did not seem very urgent; but within the last
year or two there set in an extraordinary extension of house-
building in the vicinity, in consequence of which the population has so increased that the call for a new church
seems to be imperative.

"The Presbyterial scheme for the planting of twelve new
churches, recently launched with so much success, still
further aroused our sense of duty; and finally one of our
own office-bearers, by offering to start the new enterprise
with a very large subscription, made it plain that there
was no alternative but to proceed. A very fine site has
been procured, largely through the generous intervention
of another of our office-bearers; and plans of the new
buildings are now in the course of preparation.

"We might, perhaps, have kept out of this enterprise
had we desired to do so; we might have thrown the responsibility on the Presbytery, who would have fixed upon
this, I presume, as one of their sites.

"But our congregation has long had a heavy stake in the Springbank district; and, if we are able, it will be a great satisfaction to us to plant down there an organized centre of Gospel light. Besides, we have now for a considerable number of years had great prosperity as a congregation; and it is but natural that this should embody itself in some permanent monument beyond the routine of ordinary effort. . .

"I am not sorry that the first use we are to make of our prosperity is not for ourselves, but for the public cause of the Gospel in this city; and, perhaps, if we are successful in this, other things may by-and-by be added to us."

Plans for the proposed church have since been approved, the cost has been well-nigh subscribed, and the building is already in an advanced stage. It is being erected on an admirable site close to the junction of Garscube Road and New City Road, just opposite our original rented premises, and has received the name of Queen's Cross Free Church.

On the evening of 23rd June, 1898, the ceremony of laying a memorial stone took place in presence of a large representation of office-bearers, congregation, and friends. In opening the proceedings, Dr. Stalker referred to the munificence of Mr. David Maclean, which had ensured the success of the undertaking, and to the generosity of Mr. Peter

M'Kissock, who put it in their power to secure such an advantageous site. The Rev. Dr. Whyte of Edinburgh, Moderator of the General Assembly, then laid the stone with all due formality, and thereafter addressed the company, reminding them of "the noble, ever fresh, never conventional, never common-place motto of the city, 'Let Glasgow flourish by the preaching of the Word.'" This house of prayer was a reminder to men, that if they did their work loyally as in the Great Taskmaster's eye, they would do something, for generations to come, to continue to develop and extend the prosperity, the stability and the wealth of Glasgow. Having got the church, he hoped they would also get a minister worthy of being a colleague to his friend Dr. Stalker. Psalm cxxii. 6-9 was then sung, and the assembly dispersed.

While the care of Springbank has chiefly taxed the resources of St. Matthew's, the claims of less favoured congregations who, in their own localities, are bravely seeking to solve the home mission problem, have not been entirely overlooked during those years. Opportunities have been embraced for extending needed aid, in various ways, to Springburn, Tollcross, Blochairn, Buchanan Memorial, Cranstonhill and Gorbals, in addition to which some share has been taken in the General Debt Extinction Fund.

The Psalmody Committee and Musical Association have throughout done admirable work in leading the praise at Sabbath and weeknight services, and their annual recitals have been of a high order. Special thanks were due to Mr. D. M. Munro, who, by means of a trained choir of children, and a lecture, raised sufficient money to provide the Mission with an American organ for indoor work, and a harmonium for outside. The ungrudging services of Miss Jessie Paterson as pianist upon every possible occasion at church and mission also deserve very special recognition.

In 1894 an Orchestral Society was formed in order "to bring players of instruments together for mutual improvement, with the view of helping in church and mission work when their services might be useful." This Society has given ample proof of its utility at some of the Corporation Model Lodging-houses and the Canal Boatmen's Mission, as well as at several

of our own congregational meetings, at one of
which so competent an authority as Professor
Bruce declared the rendering of " St. George's
Edinburgh " to be beyond praise.

In the same year, the Psalmody Committee
brought the question of instrumental music at
the Sabbath services before the Session, who
agreed to consult the feeling of the congregation.   Finding   that   a   very   considerable
minority were adverse, that court, with the
hearty acquiescence of all, allowed the matter
to drop.   In the present year, however, the
subject was revived by Mr. Nicholson, and the
Session, having afresh ascertained the mind of
the people, felt warranted in remitting it to
the Deacons' Court, to be dealt with in such
manner, and at such time as to their wisdom
might seem fit, on the understanding that no
debt should be incurred thereby.

In the autumn of 1889, Dr. Stalker published his first volume since coming to Glasgow.
It was entitled *Imago Christi*, and is a
devotional study of Christ's example, bearing
on the relationships of everyday life.   It had
a warm reception from the public, and was
specially interesting to ourselves as placing in

permanent form much of the teaching we had enjoyed during the preceding winters. Other important works have followed at intervals, and it is a striking proof of the favour they have met with even beyond the pale of English-speaking races, that one or another has been translated into at least seven European languages, or has found a circulation in the less easily deciphered characters of India, China and Japan.

It was with feelings of genuine satisfaction that, in 1890, the announcement was received that the University of Glasgow proposed to confer the degree of D.D. upon our minister. This was regarded as a just recognition of laborious and solid work based on ripe scholarship and wide culture. As a tangible token of the general interest in the occasion, the ladies of the congregation, by the hands of the Session-clerk, presented Dr. Stalker with the hood and cap appropriate to the degree. That he might be long spared to wear and to adorn the new dignity was the heartfelt prayer of all.

With academic laurels still green, he visited America, by invitation, in the spring of 1891 in order to deliver a course of lectures on

Preaching at Yale University. Many of these were, in substance at least, first given in St. Matthew's, and on his return the whole were published in book form, under the title of *The Preacher and his Models.* In parting with their Moderator the Session took the opportunity of expressing the hearty willingness with which they thus shared their good gift with sister churches in the New World, looking forward, however, to the time when, by God's blessing, pastor and people should again be re-united at the summer communion. In Dr. Stalker's absence the pulpit of St. Matthew's was well supplied, the Rev. Principals Caird and Rainy, Professor Laidlaw, Drs. Fergus Ferguson, Andrew Melville, Donald Macleod, Alexander Whyte and J. H. Wilson, being among those who gave willing help. Interesting letters were received from various points on the American continent, and, on the 22nd June, a hearty welcome home was accorded to Dr. and Mrs. Stalker, when the former narrated some of his experiences and impressions.

In the following year, an unsuccessful attempt was made to remove our minister to Maryle-

bone, London, in succession to the Rev.
Donald Fraser, D.D. Other proposals were
at various times mooted with the view of
securing him for Edinburgh and New York,
but absolutely unanimous representations from
his office-bearers did something, at least, to
help him to arrive at the welcome decision
to remain in Glasgow. At a large meeting
of congregational workers, held in the autumn
of 1895 in the Berkeley Hall, the ladies
presented a new pulpit gown, taking the same
opportunity of testifying affectionate regard
for Mrs. Stalker by asking her acceptance of
a drawing-room lamp.

In 1896, the Pan-Presbyterian Council met
in Glasgow, the time of their sittings coinciding
with our June communion. The Rev. Dr.
Cunningham, of Wheeling, U.S., and Principal
Rainy preached forenoon and evening, the
Revs. Wm. Park, Belfast, and Vernon Moore,
Helena, U.S., assisting Dr. Stalker by address-
ing communicants and children. Not fewer
than twenty-six of the delegates joined with
us in the service.

Sabbath, 20th June, 1897, was kept throughout the length and breadth of the land as a

day of thanksgiving to Almighty God for having spared our gracious Queen to reach her Diamond Jubilee.   In the forenoon, Dr. Stalker preached from 2 Sam. xxiii. 3-4 : "He that ruleth over men must be just, ruling in the fear of God.   And he shall be as the light of the morning, when the sun riseth, even a morning without clouds ; as the tender grass springing out of the earth by clear shining after rain."   The large congregation joined in singing "God save the Queen," not without a lump in the throat.   On Accession Day another brief service was held in the church, the Revs. A. R. MacEwen, D.D., of Claremont, and J. Brown, M.A., of St. Peter's, taking part. The joyful singing of the Bishop of Wakefield's hymn and the unanimous vocal prayer of "God save the Queen " were memorable features.

The first break in our Session by death, during the present pastorate, was the removal, on Christmas Day, 1890, of Mr. Thomas Gray, "who not only discharged with faithfulness the duties of his office, but adorned it by his character.   His enthusiasm and ripe experience were greatly valued, and he was a standing proof that genuine Christianity brightens the life, and keeps the spirit young." In 1893, Mr. Laurence Robertson was called away, "so long associated with the congregation, and for the past eight years an esteemed elder. Though lack of robust health rendered him less able than willing to take an active share in some departments of Christian work, he was felt to be a tower of strength as a wise counsellor." In 1895, the Session were called on to record "their thankful acknowledgment of Mr. Robert Craig's work of faith and labour of love while in their midst"; and in 1897, "their deep sorrow at the removal of Mr. William Kirkland,—a man of sterling character, diligent in business, fervent in spirit, serving the Lord,—one of the features of whose Christian career was his life-long devotion to Sabbath school work." Lastly, even since these sentences were penned, we have been unitedly mourning the sudden death of Mr. Peter M'Kissock, "whose shrewd, large-hearted and ever-ready counsel was felt to be simply invaluable. His own spiritual experiences had been deep and memorable, and he rejoiced in making known to others the secret which had saved and held himself."

In 1888, there passed away, in his eighty-fourth year, Mr. John B. Buchanan, a truly devoted Disruption elder of Kingston Church, who had latterly worshipped with us; and in 1889, Dr. Mackintosh, one of our oldest and most respected members, "a pioneer of new methods in a Christ-like work, which, though withdrawn from the public eye, has sensibly diminished the sum of human suffering."

Nor can we omit mention of Miss Eliza Currie, who died in 1890, "than whom no worker at Springbank has been more devoted or influential, and whose gentle presence will be sorely missed." Miss Margaret King Mitchell also was taken home in 1895. "Belonging to a family long known and highly esteemed in St. Matthew's, she was one of our most useful members, giving to the more prosaic details of missionary work-parties that skilled and careful attention which it is so difficult to replace."

We should like, in closing, to record the first wedding which had ever taken place within the walls of Free St. Matthew's. On 2nd September, 1891, Miss Lizzie MacLean, daughter of our well-known elder, was married to Mr. John B. Wallace of Liverpool. The light of her simple-hearted Christian spirit could not be hid, but shone out in every look, word and gesture. She had specially endeared herself to the young women of the congregation, as secretary of their Union. They followed her with benedictions to her new home, and it was with truly mourning hearts that, all too soon thereafter, they were called to lay a wreath of purest white flowers upon her early grave. " She is not dead, but sleepeth."

IX

St. Matthew's of To-day

.

"Walk about Zion, and go round about her; tell the towers thereof. Mark ye well her bulwarks; consider her palaces; that ye may tell it to the generation following."

PSALM xlviii. 12, 13.

St. Matthew's of To-day

IN reverting, as promised, to details of the work carried on at Springbank, there seems no way in which we can do so more naturally or satisfactorily than by inviting the reader to accompany us on a flying visit to the various agencies in operation during a single week. We shall thereafter inquire what is going on simultaneously at the church in Bath Street.

Walking out New City Road on a Sabbath morning, we find that its long stretch of hemmed-in causeway presents a very different aspect from that with which we are most familiar. Crowding and bustling have subsided for a space, and save for an occasional car toiling up to Maryhill, or a decent milk-cart, with shining pails, standing at the corner

of some cross-street, the thoroughfare is all
but clear. The unwonted quiet makes such
sylvan designations as Woodside, Well Road,
Firhill and Kelvindale sound a little less
incongruous than at other times, and helps
us to realise that these are the veritable
echoes of a bygone age, when woods and
wells, trees and dells were undeniable features
of the landscape.

Doncaster Street is already alive with children cheerily making their way to our Mission
Hall. At eleven, the Foundry Boys' Society
assembles, with an attendance of 230. Mr.
Peter Macfarlane (elder) has for some years
been the popular chairman, the infant department being presided over by Mr. A. M.
Forrester in an adjoining room. There is a
staff of about 40 monitors and a speaker is
provided by the central organization. The
teaching comprises Scripture text and lesson,
with Psalm and Shorter Catechism; prizes in
the shape of a Bible, hymn-book, or copy of
the *Pilgrim's Progress* being awarded annually
for the correct repetition of all the texts. By
means of such gatherings liberally scattered
over the city, it is calculated that sound Bibli-

cal instruction is conveyed to about 15,000
children, who might otherwise be left to lounge
at home, or loiter on the streets. It is just
possible, however, that some encouragement
is also unintentionally given to parents of
a certain class to be negligent themselves in
the matter of morning church-going, especially in the company of their families. This is
a tendency which none would desire to foster,
and we shall watch with interest an alternative
experiment, which is being tried elsewhere, of
marking and rewarding the attendance of children in the proper church of their parents.
There is a further admitted drawback in the
necessary absence of so many monitors from
the ordinary forenoon service of the sanctuary,
though to the credit of those belonging to
St. Matthew's it may well be stated that
none are more regularly in their places in
the afternoon. Moreover, their self-denying
zeal from week to week is so far beyond praise
as to entirely disarm criticism.

At a quarter-past eleven a Working Lads'
Class is held in the upper hall, under the
sympathetic presidency of Mr. Arnott. An
attractive syllabus of Bible study is in the

hands of members, rotation of speakers being arranged by Mr. Bankier, the secretary, while through the week Mr. Hunter and others give attention to the social side and to visitation. A sight of those sixty or seventy eager, upturned faces, with the opportunity of hearing their lusty singing, amply rewards a visit, which, we are assured, is always welcome. It is quite impossible to look upon this stalwart band without reflecting that there must be many in it who are "not far from the kingdom," or without longing to see it become more unmistakably a recruiting ground for open profession and church membership. In a recently published account of the Pleasance Mission in Edinburgh, it is mentioned that for many years ten to fifteen young communicants were regularly drawn from an exactly similar source. How encouraging to all concerned would such a harvest be!

At a quarter-past two, there is a service in the hall, conducted by the missionary, and attended by about sixty persons gathered from the district.

The Sabbath school opens at half-past five. It has been fortunate in having had, from the first, a succession of able office-bearers as superintendents, Mr. Buist (elder) at present acting in that capacity. Here we find some 380 children and 30 or 40 teachers in actual attendance, and we fancy that few schools in the city are better equipped. With the younger children separated, and ten or twelve detached class-rooms for the more grown-up boys and girls, the outward conditions for effective teaching seem highly favourable.

At seven o'clock the chief adult service of the day is held, conducted by the missionary assistant. It is preceded by a short open-air gathering, and is well attended. The Lord's Supper is, by authority of the Presbytery, dispensed quarterly, the present membership being 114. On these occasions a number of Free St. Matthew's members are always present. The praise, under the enthusiastic leadership of Mr. Menmuir, is peculiarly hearty, many of our best singers lending willing help in this way. That the people may be trained in Christian giving, collections are taken monthly for the Sustentation Fund, and quarterly for Foreign Missions, in addition to the ordinary church plate.

These have yielded, for the past year, £4 12s. 7d. and £1 4s. respectively. It should be added that two elders—at present Messrs. John Bryce and J. S. Gregson—are detailed for the more immediate supervision of the district. These, with the Missionary Assistant and Bible-woman, form a kind of permanent committee which can advise the Session in cases of application for membership or of discipline.

On nearly every evening of the week the halls are fully engaged.

Monday is a stirring night. At an early hour the doors are besieged by the thrifty and intellectual sections of our young people. The Savings Bank, under the charge of Mr. W. O. Small, registers 7800 transactions in a year, representing over £300 in deposits. The Library issues from forty to fifty volumes weekly, from a nominal stock of several hundreds; but as the books by-and-by get worn out, not to speak of becoming antiquated, additions are very acceptable. A Reading-room, well supplied with weekly papers and monthly magazines, is also thrown open to members of the Young Men's class.

In the hall, Mr. Robert Leisk conducts an encouraging Band of Hope, with about sixty members.

On Tuesday the week-night service for adults is held in the hall, with a fair attendance. Upstairs the Christian Endeavour Society assembles in two sections, the senior being led by Messrs. Peter Macfarlane and J. S. Gregson, the junior by Miss Kenneth. That of St. Matthew's Mission was the first branch to be started in Glasgow, and has been found a potent factor for good. Its motto is " For Christ and the Church," and it is composed of "young people who have been led to trust the Lord Jesus as their Saviour, and who desire to show their love to Him by serving Him every day." Discussion has lately arisen as to the utility of this new organization in church life. Now, while this must ever depend upon the wisdom of those who guide, it would be strange indeed if the central ideas underlying so remarkable a movement could not be assimilated, without placing a fictitious value on merely accidental details. In our case there need not be the slightest misgiving, so long as we have such devoted

M

elders at the helm. At the same time, we do well to ask ourselves with regard to all our methods, if we may not rest too easily satisfied with being consciously instructive, without making sure that we are also, in the truest sense, constructive. Is it not the fact that we are often more attentive to note, and more careful to tabulate, the numbers enrolled in each of our initiatory departments than to inquire how many are ultimately led by their means into the fixed habit of church attendance, and into the intelligent desire for church membership? Yet these are the ends that should never be lost sight of; these are results which, if attained, would demonstrate utility beyond question. In this view it is gratifying to know that several members of the Christian Endeavour Society are at present attending a preparatory class with the intention of seeking admission to the Lord's Table.

On Wednesday afternoon our Bible-woman holds her Mothers' Meeting, and this is certainly one of the most flourishing institutions at Springbank. About sixty mothers attend regularly, and although Miss Campbell is always a host in herself, she welcomes the valuable help given by several ladies in the congregation. In the evening, the Choir holds its practice, and a Gymnasium is likewise thrown open for the benefit of the young men.

Thursday is a day of diffused effort throughout the district. Eight Kitchen Meetings, arranged for by Mr. Gumprecht, are conducted by as many office-bearers and others in the homes of the people, and in connection with these a large staff of Tract Distributors, superintended by Mr. Steel, visits the different stairs. In these ways acquaintance with the circumstances of the families is acquired, and many opportunities for sympathy and timely aid naturally present themselves. Meantime, the Girls' Union is in possession of the hall, and here sewing is taught, relieved by occasional demonstrations in cookery, laundry work, etc. The Union has from the first been singularly fortunate in its presidents, Miss Macfadzean, Miss Cree, and Mrs. Peter Macfarlane having successively rendered admirable service.

On Friday, the 12th company of the Boys' Brigade assembles for drill, and a thoroughly presentable contingent it makes, with its smart uniform, and the bright faces of its members, well worthy to share in the commendation bestowed by Lord Roberts upon the Glasgow battalions. Mr. Archibald Kennedy holds the post of captain in succession to Messrs. William Black and Alexander Leitch.

On Saturday there has usually been a Gospel Temperance meeting, conducted on lines varying from year to year. This, however, is at present in abeyance, affording a welcome breathing time to our worthy hall-keeper in view of Sabbath.

Of occasional meetings, we must specially mention the solemn Watch-night Service with which each New Year is ushered in; the bright and crowded gathering of happy children at noon on the same day; and the great annual Flower Show held every autumn. This last, indeed, is an event of such outstanding interest in the mission calendar that we must transcribe a few paragraphs from a descriptive sketch which appeared in one of the *Monthly* supplements.

"By three o'clock about eighty plants had been entered by the children for competition, and an equal number had been received on loan from the Corporation and from helpers in the church. Shortly afterwards the judge arrived and the children's plants were carefully and patiently passed under review, now with a word of special commendation and now with a kindly hint how to improve; and when at last the prizes were awarded and the flowers all placed in position, the hall presented such an appearance as the oldest inhabitant had seldom seen. At half-past six the doors were opened, and in streamed an expectant crowd of boys and girls. It did one's heart good to hear the involuntary and expressive "Oh!" burst in chorus from each fresh batch of arrivals, and to see the excitement and joy stamped on every feature. The sense of proprietorship too gave a touch of pride and eagerness to the happy faces; for was it not their own flower show for the success of which they had been working night and morning for months? It was a real luxury to wander about, and to be gently dragged from table to table to admire the beauties of this geranium or that fuchsia, and to hear how they had watched its growth all through the summer, and how many blossoms it had shown at one time."

On the following day, some of the flowers are distributed throughout the district, while others go perhaps to cheer little sufferers in the Sick Children's Hospital. All through the summer, indeed, a fortnightly distribution takes place among the sick and aged, timely intimation of the dates when flowers are received for this purpose being given on the *Record* cover.

But it is now high time that we were turning our steps towards St. Matthew's itself, from whence the motive power for all these organizations is derived, and where we shall find a similar activity pervading the entire week. In making ourselves acquainted with the work carried on there, we cannot do better than follow the plan which we have adopted at Springbank, though in this case we propose to reserve Sabbath to the last, not as a reversion to Jewish practice, but because that day is a high day—the best of all the seven.

Let us then commence our visitation on a Monday evening, going down early so as to have time for a look round before others have gathered. As we thread our way by Charing Cross, with its meshes of tramway rails, its constant stream of traffic, and its glare of electric light, we are reminded in how many ways the neighbourhood has altered since the times referred to in our opening chapter. And yet as we turn into Newton Street, and see the stately spire of St. Matthew's clear against the clouds, a spirit of restfulness possesses us, and we feel that we are still on familiar ground. The open gate in front and the lighted lamp within indicate sufficiently that business is on hand.

We are met at the door by Thomas Herd, who has been church officer for fifteen years, and who can put us up to anything we want to know. He carries a directory of the congregation in the back of his head, and has early information on most subjects. He shows us at once into the Deacons' Court Room with a cheerful fire already ablaze. The massive oak frame above the mantel-piece, enclosing fifty or sixty cabinet photographs, was the gift of Mr. David MacLean in 1890, and represents the entire Deacons' Court as it then stood. It may be mentioned in this connection that our elder, Mr. Currie, has long had the idea that an interesting collection of ecclesiastical portraits might adorn our halls, if members and friends would only send in such as they were willing to part with, and which are sometimes even relegated to the lumber room at home. A beginning has already been made with—

D. O. Hill's Disruption Assembly.
Allan's General Assembly of 1787.
First Meeting of Secession Fathers at Gairney Bridge in 1733.
Portrait of Dr. John Erskine of Greyfriars (immortalized by Scott in *Guy Mannering*).

Portrait of Dr. Andrew Thomson of St. George's,
Edinburgh.
Portrait of Dr. Inglis of Edinburgh (father of late
Lord President Inglis).
Portrait of Sir H. Moncrieff Wellwood (grandfather
of the late Baronet, Clerk of Assembly).
Portraits of our own Apostolic succession : Dr. Samuel
Miller, Dr. John Watson, Rev. C. A. Salmond,
M.A., Dr. James Stalker.

Soon after half-past seven the collectors drop
in with Sustentation and Foreign Mission contributions, reporting their successes or dis-
appointments, with zealous solicitude, to the
respective treasurers. We are quite certain
that could our members but witness the arrival
of these faithful auxiliaries—perhaps with drip-
ping garments on a winter night,—they would
appreciate in a new way how much the church
owes to such unobtrusive service, and would
make a point of lightening the labours of
their rounds by a kindly welcome or a sealed
envelope in waiting. At eight o'clock, the
Deacons' Court meets for ordinary business,
taking up, as a fixed item on the agenda
paper for each month, the report of one of its
standing committees.

In the large hall, the Young Women's Union

meets on alternate Mondays, and, with that
turn for practicality combined with variety
which distinguishes the sex, seems equally
happy in cutting out rudimentary clothing for
Galla boys and famine orphans, or in listening
to music, travellers' tales, or missionary intelli-
gence. Nor must we omit mention of the
Ladies' Work Association, composed of the
wives of office-bearers and others, which con-
sults together once a month on this afternoon.
Its chief objects are the visitation of sick
and lonely ones both of church and mission,
the sympathetic superintendence of the Bible-
woman's work and the support of our lady
missionary in India.

On Tuesday evenings the Young Men's
Literary Society is in session, and there
governments are made and unmade, the
relative positions in literature of Tennyson
and Browning are definitely ascertained, and
the more outlying portions of the globe
are ransacked by the aid of lime-light,—all
within elders' hours. When a lecturer of
outstanding interest has been captured either
by this Society, or by the Young Women's
Union, a joint meeting is arranged, and is

thrown open to the congregation. Dr. Stalker
has been in the habit of giving, for the
benefit of both, an annual study of some poet's
teaching—Burns, Tennyson, and Shakespeare
in various moods, being memorable examples.

Wednesday night is devoted to the Prayer
Meeting, committees being usually called,
for convenience, before or after. It is held
in the church, the area of which is largely
filled. Promptly at eight o'clock, Dr. Stalker
steps on the platform, which is the signal for
the choir to collect the thoughts of the congregation by singing an appropriate Scripture
Sentence. Prayer and praise thereafter alternate for half an hour, two office-bearers or
other friends invariably taking part. A carefully prepared and suggestive address follows, and the meeting disperses before nine
o'clock has struck. The Psalms afforded ample
subject of meditation for nine successive
winters, two from the first hundred being
alternated with one from the latter fifty; and
as the triumphal symphony of the closing
Psalm died away, it was with a sense of regret
that we could not just begin over again. The
gracious words which proceeded out of the

mouth of Christ are now being taken up in order, and the Sermon on the Mount has alone been found a mine of unfathomable depth. At intervals an evening has been spared for the consideration of missionary subjects, the lives of great hymn-writers, family worship, and temperance. The Session statedly meets at the close of the prayer meeting on the second Wednesday of each month and oftener as required.

On alternate Thursdays the Orchestral Society holds its practisings, while the free night is much in demand for social re-unions of one kind or another. The Total Abstinence Society endeavours to arrange two or three such gatherings in the course of the winter.

On Friday evening there is a Children's Praise Meeting at a quarter before seven, followed by the Psalmody Association at eight o'clock. At each of these there is generally the systematic study of some sacred cantata in addition to the practice of anthems and other more familiar church music.

Owing to the conveniently west-central position of our church halls, the use of them is frequently asked and willingly granted for

non-congregational purposes, such as meetings
of the Women's Foreign Missionary Association, Sabbath School Union and other societies,
so that it will be seen that they are pretty
fully occupied.

Coming now to the Sabbath day, it may
be stated that we adhere to the usual forenoon
and afternoon diets of worship, nor is there
anything in the attendances at either to indicate that change would be of advantage.
Both are large—especially, perhaps, that of
the afternoon.

The ordinary services are preceded by
gatherings of the Young Men's and Young
Women's Fellowship Unions, and are followed
by the Sabbath School and Bible Class. The
first of these has a carefully drawn syllabus,
calling for strenuous study on the part of
members in turn. Mr. MacLean has long
thrown his whole heart into this work, and
it was only the other day that the grateful
feelings of the young men found vent in the
presentation to him of a beautifully illuminated
address. The Sabbath School assembles at
half-past five, and has been for many years
under the superintendence of Mr. Watt, elder.

There is an attendance of about 120 scholars and 17 teachers. The Bible Class is taught by the assistant for the time being, and subjects prescribed by the Welfare of Youth Committee are usually taken up. There are seventy to eighty on the roll.

Once a month Dr. Stalker preaches a Children's Sermon in the forenoon, and in the afternoon gives one of a course of lectures "intended chiefly for those who, through being engaged at the children's church or in similar work in the forenoon, miss the regular morning lecture." The subjects thus taken up have been very varied, and have included "The Teaching of Christ according to the Synoptical Gospels," "The Poetry of the Old Testament," "Jeremiah, the Man and his Message," "Religious Psychology," "Conversion illustrated in the Lives of Saintly Men, from Augustine to Rabbi Duncan," and "The Background of the Life of Christ." It is superfluous to say that they have been in the highest degree informing to those who themselves seek to impart to others. At the ordinary forenoon service lecturing has been the rule. Biblical history and biography, Christian

doctrine and interpretation have each in turn
yielded abundant material "profitable for instruction in righteousness." The short courses
dealing with the lives of "Joseph," "St. Peter,"
"The Two St. Johns," "The Essentials and
Non-essentials of Christianity," "The Parables
of Zechariah," and "The Parables of our
Lord," as well as the longer one on "The
Trial and Death of Jesus," will be gratefully
remembered by different sections of the congregation. In the afternoon we have most
commonly a sermon, with its divisions dis-
tinctly stated at the outset from a small slip
of paper which is seldom again referred to.

While it would be out of place to attempt
to characterize the preaching with which we
are so highly favoured, we may at least be
allowed to say that it is both suggestive and
stimulating in a remarkable degree. With
the true instinct of an interpreter, the preacher
seems to place himself alongside his hearers,
accurately gauging their standpoint, and leading up therefrom to the inculcation of highest
doctrine stated in untechnical but purposeful
language. He comes charged with a message
from God, which he delivers sympathetically,

yet with no uncertain sound. All ages, classes, and temperaments, with their questionings, burdens, and temptations, are kept in view, and it is shown how the gospel has a practical lesson for each. Those who most regularly wait upon this ministry are best able to appreciate the many-sided aspects of truth which are thus naturally and systematically unfolded from the Word of God. We cannot for a moment doubt that in the Spirit's hand it is often used for turning many to righteousness, and in building up many more in their most holy faith.

It is with satisfaction that the congregation has just learned of Dr. Stalker's appointment as Cunningham Lecturer for 1899, when it is understood that his subject will be *Christ's Teaching about Himself*.

The sacrament of baptism is now administered near the commencement of public worship, and this arrangement has certainly the advantage of fixing the hour when the mother's presence is required, and of setting the minds of both parents free to enjoy other parts of the service. The congregation stand during the dispensation of the ordin-

ance, and at its conclusion spontaneously join
in the unanimous prayer :

"The Lord bless thee, and keep thee :
The Lord make His face shine upon thee, and be
gracious unto thee :
The Lord lift up His countenance upon thee, and give
thee peace."

With the view of simplifying arrangements
and of promoting that quiet which is in itself
so helpful, the entire afternoon is devoted to
the Quarterly Communion Service, the action
sermon and fencing of the tables being given
earlier in the day.   Great pains have also been
taken, in the spirit of Christ's own example
when feeding the multitude, to secure the
utmost precision on the part of officiating elders,
so that no avoidable distraction may mar the
solemn feast.   A card of minute instructions
has been drawn up, which has been found
to serve its purpose well, and not a few testi-
monies have been borne by strangers to the
impressiveness of the sight from the platform
of eight hundred communicants with one ac-
cord celebrating the Lord's death.

As these occasions are undoubtedly the most
memorable in St. Matthew's, we should like

Free St. Matthew's Church, Glasgow.

Communion, _____ 189___

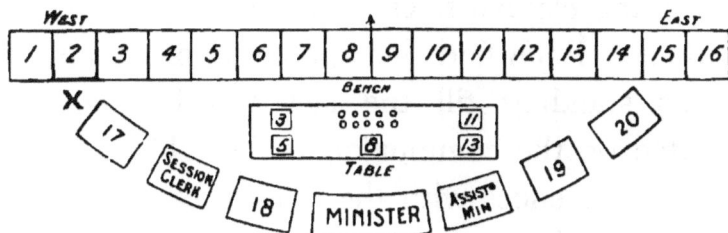

WEST → EAST

| 1 | 2 | 3 | 4 | 5 | 6 | 7 | 8 | 9 | 10 | 11 | 12 | 13 | 14 | 15 | 16 |

BENCH

Mr. _____

The **X** indicates Seat to be occupied.

Elements should be placed on Table in position shewn.

Each Elder will kindly study back of Card, so as to make himself familiar with duty assigned

Elders unable to be present should advise Session-Clerk in advance.

All others should wait for instructions at close of Preparatory Service.

Order of Service.

Officiating Elders, unless required earlier, should be in West room by 1·50 p.m. At 2 o'clock they enter Church by East door, following Minister in order called by Clerk.

After depositing their charge on Communion Table, they remain standing opposite seats assigned until all the Elements have been placed on Table. *At the words of Institution* all rise simultaneously, but only step on platform in turn as required. All stand during praise and prayer.

The serving Elders are themselves served after the Congregation.

Immediately after Benediction has been pronounced, the Elders remove the Elements by West door, following Minister in same order as on entering.

Care should be taken throughout that corresponding Elders on either side of Church keep as nearly as possible opposite each other.

[P.T.O.

ELDERS' CARD OF INSTRUCTIONS (Front).

FREE CHURCH OF SCOTLAND

HOC TAMEN CONSUMEBATUR

FREE ST MATTHEW'S CHURCH, GLASGOW. 1843.

THIS DO IN REMEMBRANCE OF ME

I COR. XI. 24

ST. MATTHEW'S TOKEN (Now disused).

to set down briefly the order of service. At two o'clock, Dr. Stalker and the assisting minister, followed by a large company of elders bearing the elements, enter the church by the east door. Each finds his appointed place, and remains standing till the last cup has been deposited on the communion table. Then the service commences with the full-voiced singing of that exalted strain of Zion :

> "O send Thy light forth and Thy truth;
>   Let them be guides to me,
> And bring me to Thine holy hill,
>   Even where Thy dwellings be.
> Then will I to God's altar go,
>   To God my chiefest joy:
> Yea, God, my God, Thy name to praise
>   My harp I will employ."

A short passage of Scripture and prayer follow, and the familiar 35th Paraphrase is sung, ending with those fine lines which sum up, almost in Christ's own words, the spirit and import of the ordinance :

> "With love to man this cup is fraught,
>   Let all partake the sacred draught;
> Through latest ages let it pour,
>   In mem'ry of My dying hour."

Authority having been read from 1 Cor.,
chap. xi., and the thanksgiving prayer offered,
a brief address is given, after which the symbols
of dying love are distributed, and a hushed
silence falls upon the great congregation, broken
only by the footsteps of the elders passing
from pew to pew. Returning to the platform,
the officiating elders are served by other
brethren, and then all give expression to their
pent-up feelings in that most appropriate of
communion hymns by our own Bonar :

"Here, O my Lord, I see Thee face to face;
    Here would I touch and handle things unseen,
    Here grasp with firmer hand the eternal grace,
    And all my weariness upon Thee lean.

Here would I feed upon the bread of God,
    Here drink with Thee the royal wine of heaven;
    Here would I lay aside each earthly load,
    Here taste afresh the calm of sin forgiven.

This is the hour of banquet and of song;
    This is the heavenly table spread for me;
    Here let me feast, and, feasting, still prolong
    The brief, bright hour of fellowship with Thee."

The assisting minister follows with an address,
at the close of which a few words on the "meaning of this service" are spoken by Dr. Stalker

to the expectant children in the side galleries, and after prayer the whole concludes with the last verses of the same hymn :

"Too soon we rise; the symbols disappear;
    The feast, though not the love, is past and gone;
The bread and wine remove, but Thou art here,
    Nearer than ever, still my shield and sun.

Feast after feast thus comes and passes by,
    Yet, passing, points to the glad feast above,
Giving sweet foretaste of the festal joy,
    The Lamb's great bridal feast of bliss and love."

Thus do we approach the sacred ordinance by the gateway of prophetic aspiration, and, looking through the lattice of the Upper Room, behold the Saviour in the very act of institution. As we endeavour to realize, in our own experience, some true communion with Himself and with His saints, we seem to be "compassed about with a great cloud of witnesses." Our hearts burn within us as we call to mind "the goodly company of the apostles, the noble army of martyrs, the holy church throughout all the world,"—guests like us at the same table, spread for disciples till the end of time. Others there are besides, who are never far from our thoughts,—loved ones of our own,—

who used to sit beside us at this feast, and pass to us the cup of blessing. Musing on their absence now, our sorrow is turned into joy, as we remember how they "have washed their robes, and made them white in the blood of the Lamb. Therefore are they before the throne of God."

> "Now with triumphal palms they stand
> Before the throne on high,
> And serve the God they love, amidst
> The glories of the sky."

It is with hallowed strains like these echoing around us that we should choose to close this brief record of St. Matthew's; yet ought we not first to acknowledge from the heart our gratitude to God for all His great goodness to us, as a congregation, during the four successive ministries we have been recalling? And as we wistfully turn towards the future, longing for some assurance that He who hath been mindful of us will still bless us, do we not catch a whispered message from the Master Himself, who, while taking us into His confidence, would at the same time acquaint us with the conditions of His favour: "If ye abide in Me, and My words abide in you, ye shall ask what ye will, and it shall be done unto you"?   Let us, therefore, who name ourselves *of Zion*, see that we be "holy, every one written among the living in Jerusalem"; and let us not cease to pray for her prosperity. Then may "the children of Zion be joyful in their King," for to them shall be fulfilled the promise that is written :

> "I will abundantly bless her provision,
> I will satisfy her poor with bread,
> Her priests will I clothe with salvation,
> And her saints shall shout aloud for joy."

☩

For my brethren and companions' sakes
I will now say,
Peace be within thee.

X
Appendix

Office-Bearers of Free St. Matthew's

(1) ELDERS.

Those marked * are still in office.

Ordained or Inducted.		Ordained or Inducted.	
1840	Allan Buchanan.	1861	James Macarthur.
1840	James Keyden.	1861	William Allan.
1841	Peter Lawson.	1861	John Muir.
1842	David Stow.	1865	George Reith.
1844	Alexander Wingate.	1865	Gilbert Beith.
1846	Hugh Cogan.	1865	David Hay.
1846	William Cumming.	1865	James C. Wyper.
1846	Robert Forrester.	1865	John Boag.
1847	Andrew Nielson.	1865	William Ramsay.
1847	John Wilson.	1865	James Miller.
1847	George M. Sandilands.	1865	Thomas Wharrie.
1848	Robert Fleming.	1868	James White.
1848	John Thomson.	1868	Neil Caw.
1848	Thomas L. Paterson.	1868	James Connell.
1848	Plummer Dewar.	1868	Robert King.
1848	William Mirrlees.	1868	William Fairbairn.
1852	James Wright.	1868	William Mathison.
1852	William Mackinlay.	1868	John A. Mathieson.
1852	Francis J. Ferguson.	1868	Walter Scobie.
1852	Archibald M'Nicol.	1876	Donald M'Calman.
1852	Thomas M'Micking.	1876	James Guthrie.
1852	William Paul.	1876	William Kirkland.
1855	George Adam.	1876	*Robert W. Anderson.
1855	David C. Nichol.	1876	Walter S. Hislop.
1855	Robert B. Park.	1880	*James Imrie.
1858	Robert Burns.	1880	George M. Grierson.
1858	John Duncan.	1880	James Glass.
1858	Neil M'Master.	1880	*James M'Michael.
1861	John King.	1880	*David Pratt.
1861	Michael Honeyman.	1880	Henry A. Rannie.

Ordained or Inducted.		Ordained or Inducted.	
1880	*James B. Steel.	1891	Robert Craig.
1880	Ebenezer Watson, M.D.	1891	*William R. Currie.
1880	Robert Vanhegan.	1891	*William Sinclair.
1883	Robert E. Aitken.	1891	William Nielson.
1883	Thomas Gray.	1891	William Lindsay.
1883	Robert D. Macalister.	1891	Walter G. Steven.
1883	John Macfarlane.	1893	*John Boyd.
1883	John Munro.	1893	*John Gumprecht.
1883	*George E. Philip.	1893	*William M. Harvey.
1883	Laurence Robertson.	1893	*Peter Macfarlane.
1883	Thomas M. Welsh.	1893	*James Nicholson.
1885	David Clow.	1893	*Thomas Noble.
1885	Matthew Edwards.	1893	*A. Wood Smith, M.D.
1885	*John Fulton.	1895	*William Bennett.
1885	*Robert Russell.	1895	*John Bryce.
1885	*John W. J. Watt.	1895	*John S. Gregson.
1885	*Robert Mackintosh.	1895	*John Hunter.
1888	*David MacLean.	1895	John Masson.
1888	*Archd. Macfarlane.	1895	*James Millar.
1888	Peter M'Kissock.	1895	Finlay Macleod.
1888	*Robert Scott.	1897	*Alexander Bissett.
1888	R. W. Ralston.	1897	*David Gordon.
1891	Ebenezer Alexander.	1897	*Andrew Lawrie.
1891	William Black.	1897	*Frederick A. Laing.
1891	*James Buist.	1897	*James H. Meikle.

(2) DEACONS.

1844	William Mirrlees.	1846	William Craies.
1844	Walter B. Ogilvie.	1848	Francis J. Ferguson.
1844	George Murray.	1848	Jesse Jones.
1844	John Adam.	1848	Robert Cross.
1844	William Freebairn.	1848	William Ramsay.
1846	Robert Hamilton.	1850	Robert B. Park.
1846	J. B. Mirrlees.	1850	John M'Kundy.
1846	John Currie.	1850	Archibald M'Nicol.

Ordained or Inducted.		Ordained or Inducted.	
1850	Robert Vanhegan.	1869	William M'Isaac.
1853	James Campbell.	1869	William Stewart.
1853	Michael Honeyman.	1869	David Greig.
1853	Thomas Sprunt.	1869	Robert Bishop.
1853	John W. Robertson.	1869	Patrick Robertson.
1853	William Allan.	1869	Henry Forrester.
1853	David C. Nichol.	1869	Robert H. Robertson.
1853	William Church.	1869	John M'Kendrick.
1853	John Church.	1869	James Imrie.
1853	Neil M'Master.	1877	Peter M'Kichan.
1853	John Muir.	1877	*Robert S. Buchanan.
1853	John Macarthur.	1877	*William Miller.
1856	Robert Urquhart.	1877	James B. Steel.
1856	James P. Miller.	1877	James F. Barron.
1856	John A. Matheson.	1877	John M'Kill.
1856	George Craik.	1877	James Jack.
1856	John Boag.	1877	John W. Weir, M.D.
1856	Walter G. Maclaren.	1877	Jonathan Armour.
1859	Robert Blackie.	1877	Thomas M. Welsh.
1859	Neil Caw.	1877	James Glass.
1859	Archibald Grierson.	1877	Alexander M'Lennan.
1859	Adam M. Pattison.	1880	Alexander M'Kill.
1859	Robert Gilkison.	1880	William Black.
1859	Thomas Wharrie.	1880	Robert M'Kill.
1861	Robert King.	1880	*Robert Bissett.
1861	James Connell.	1880	Robert D. Macalister.
1861	Timothy Bost.	1880	John Munro.
1861	George M. Grierson.	1880	William R. Currie.
1861	John Williamson.	1880	W. F. Maclaren.
1865	James Grierson.	1880	*Alexander Cameron.
1865	David Lawson.	1880	James Nicholson.
1865	William L. Watson.	1883	David F. Anderson.
1865	George Young.	1883	*Henry Blackhall.
1865	Alexander Stephen.	1883	Alexander B. Kirsop.
1865	John Honeyman, Jr.	1883	William Miller, Jr.
1869	William M'Callum.	1883	*Robert Montgomery.
1869	John Currie.	1883	Daniel Macintyre.

Ordained or Inducted.		Ordained or Inducted.	
1883	*James M'Michael, Jr.	1892	*James Welsh.
1883	*Andrew Parker.	1892	*Thomas S. Young.
1883	Hugh Ross.	1893	David Gordon.
1883	James A. Small.	1893	John Masson.
1883	John W. J. Watt.	1893	William Bennett.
1885	*Robert Love.	1893	Herbert C. Boyd.
1885	Peter Macfarlane.	1893	*Alex. K. Foote.
1885	*George D. Marr.	1893	John Hunter.
1885	Donald M. Munro.	1893	*Alexander Leitch.
1885	William Sandilands.	1893	*John Macdonald.
1885	William Tait.	1893	*A. N. Macgregor, M.D.
1885	*James Thomson.	1893	*Charles S. Macintyre.
1885	Alexander Walker.	1893	John M. M'Kendrick.
1885	John Wilson.	1893	*John Stewart.
1889	John Black.	1896	*Alexander Bayne.
1889	John Boyd.	1896	*Alexander M. Forrester.
1889	William M. Harvey.	1896	*Alexander Gerrard.
1889	*William Hislop.	1896	*A. Cowan Holburn.
1889	*Alexander Kerr.	1896	*Joseph Menmuir.
1889	*Robert Lawrie.	1896	*James H. Nicoll, M.D.
1889	Archibald Macniven.	1896	*John T. Robertson.
1889	Thomas Noble.	1896	Andrew Robbie.
1889	*Thomas M. Pratt.	1896	*Alexander Ralston.
1889	George Tudhope.	1896	*William O. Small.
1892	Alexander Cleghorn.	1896	*William Watson.
1892	David L. Forgan.	1896	*William Weatherston.
1892	John S. Gregson.	1898	*Samuel Bankier.
1892	*William Greig, Jr.	1898	*W. T. H. Coutts.
1892	John Gumprecht.	1898	*George Lang.
1892	Andrew Macfadzean.	1898	*Robert Leisk.
1892	*Robert M'Millan.	1898	*Robert M'Eachran.
1892	*Robert C. Morgan.	1898	*James M'Ewen.
1892	Arnold Morton.	1898	*Donald M'Niven.
1892	James D. Renwick.	1898	*Charles M'Phater.
1892	*David Rintoul.	1898	*Laur. V. G. Robertson.
1892	*Matthew Walker.	1898	*Robert P. Wright.
1892	William Wallace.		

Year.	Minister.	Session Clerk.	Deacons' Court Clerk.
1844	Samuel Miller.	James Keyden.	William Mirrlees.
1845	Samuel Miller.	James Keyden.	William Mirrlees.
1846	Samuel Miller.	{ James Keyden. Wm. Cumming.	William Mirrlees.
1847	Samuel Miller.	Wm. Cumming.	William Mirrlees.
1848	Samuel Miller, D.D.	Wm. Cumming.	William Mirrlees.
1849	Samuel Miller, D.D.	Wm. Cumming.	William Mirrlees.
1850	Samuel Miller, D.D.	Wm. Cumming.	{ William Mirrlees. Jesse Jones.
1851	Samuel Miller, D.D.	Wm. Cumming.	Jesse Jones.
1852	Samuel Miller, D.D.	Wm. Cumming.	{ Jesse Jones. Andrew Nielson.
1853	Samuel Miller, D.D.	Wm. Cumming.	Andrew Nielson.
1854	Samuel Miller, D.D.	Wm. Cumming.	Andrew Nielson.
1855	Samuel Miller, D.D.	Wm. Cumming.	Andrew Nielson.
1856	Samuel Miller, D.D.	Wm. Cumming.	Andrew Nielson.
1857	Samuel Miller, D.D.	Wm. Cumming.	William Allan.
1858	Samuel Miller, D.D.	Wm. Cumming.	{ William Allan. James Macarthur.
1859	Samuel Miller, D.D.	Wm. Cumming.	James Macarthur.
1860	Samuel Miller, D.D.	Wm. Cumming.	James Macarthur.
1861	Samuel Miller, D.D.	Wm. Cumming.	James Macarthur.
1862	Samuel Miller, D.D.	Wm. Cumming.	James Macarthur.
1863	Samuel Miller, D.D.	Wm. Cumming.	James Macarthur.
1864	Samuel Miller, D.D.	Wm. Cumming.	James Macarthur.
1865	Samuel Miller, D.D.	Wm. Cumming.	James Macarthur.
1866	Samuel Miller, D.D.	Wm. Cumming.	{ James Macarthur. Wm. L. Watson.
1867	Samuel Miller, D.D.	Wm. Cumming.	Wm. L. Watson.
1868	Samuel Miller, D.D.	Wm. Cumming.	Wm. L. Watson.
1869	Samuel Miller, D.D.	Wm. Cumming.	Wm. L. Watson.
1870	Samuel Miller, D.D.	Wm. Cumming.	Wm. L. Watson.
1871	Samuel Miller, D.D.	Wm. Cumming.	Wm. L. Watson.

Congregational Treasurer.	Sustentation Treasurer.	Foreign Missions Treasurer.	Year.
{ Allan Buchanan. William Mirrlees.	Allan Buchanan.		1844
William Mirrlees.	John Adam.		1845
William Mirrlees.	John Adam.	No	1846
William Mirrlees.	John Adam.	Association	1847
William Mirrlees.	John Adam.	till	1848
William Mirrlees.	John Adam.		1849
William Mirrlees.	F. J. Ferguson.	1852.	1850
{ William Mirrlees. Archibald M'Nicol.	F. J. Ferguson.		1851
Archibald M'Nicol.	F. J. Ferguson.	Thos. M'Micking.	1852
Archibald M'Nicol.	F. J. Ferguson.	Thos. M'Micking.	1853
William Church.	F. J. Ferguson.	Thos. M'Micking.	1854
William Church.	F. J. Ferguson.	{ Thos. M'Micking. Robert B. Park.	1855
William Church.	F. J. Ferguson.	Robert B. Park.	1856
William Church.	F. J. Ferguson.	Robert B. Park.	1857
William Church.	F. J. Ferguson.	Robert B. Park.	1858
William Church.	F. J. Ferguson.	Robert B. Park.	1859
William Church.	F. J. Ferguson.	Robert B. Park.	1860
William Church.	F. J. Ferguson.	Robert B. Park.	1861
William Church.	F. J. Ferguson.	Robert B. Park.	1862
William Church.	F. J. Ferguson.	Archd. Grierson.	1863
William Church.	F. J. Ferguson.	Archd. Grierson.	1864
William Church.	F. J. Ferguson.	Archd. Grierson.	1865
William Church.	F. J. Ferguson.	Archd. Grierson.	1866
William Church.	F. J. Ferguson.	Archd. Grierson.	1867
William Church.	F. J. Ferguson.	Archd. Grierson.	1868
William Church.	F. J. Ferguson.	James C. Wyper.	1869
William Church.	{ F. J. Ferguson. Neil Caw.	James C. Wyper.	1870
William Church.	Neil Caw.	William Ramsay.	1871

Year.	Minister.	Session Clerk.	Deacons' Court Clerk.
1872	Samuel Miller, D.D.	Wm. Cumming.	{ Wm. L. Watson. James Grierson.
1873	Samuel Miller, D.D.	Wm. Cumming.	James Grierson.
1874	Samuel Miller, D.D.	Wm. Cumming.	James Grierson.
1875	Samuel Miller, D.D.	{ Wm. Cumming. William Allan.	James Grierson.
1876	Samuel Miller, D.D.	{ Wm. Cumming. William Allan.	{ James Grierson. Robt. W. Anderson.
1877	{ Samuel Miller, D.D. John Watson, M.A.	Thomas Wharrie.	Robt. W. Anderson.
1878	{ Samuel Miller, D.D. John Watson, M.A.	Thomas Wharrie.	Robt. W. Anderson.
1879	{ Samuel Miller, D.D. John Watson, M.A.	Thomas Wharrie.	Robt. W. Anderson.
1880	{ Samuel Miller, D.D. John Watson, M.A.	Thomas Wharrie.	Robt. W. Anderson.
1881	{ Samuel Miller, D.D. C. A. Salmond, M.A.	Thomas Wharrie.	Robt. W. Anderson.
1882	C. A. Salmond, M.A.	Thomas Wharrie.	Robt. W. Anderson.
1883	C. A. Salmond, M.A.	Thomas Wharrie.	{ Jonathan Armour. Jas. M'Michael, Jr.
1884	C. A. Salmond, M.A.	Thomas Wharrie.	Jas. M'Michael, Jr.
1885	C. A. Salmond, M.A.	Thomas Wharrie.	Jas. M'Michael, Jr.
1886	C. A. Salmond, M.A.	Thomas Wharrie.	Jas. M'Michael, Jr.
1887	James Stalker, M.A.	{ Thomas Wharrie. George E. Philip.	Jas. M'Michael, Jr.
1888	James Stalker, M.A.	George E. Philip.	Jas. M'Michael, Jr.
1889	James Stalker, M.A.	George E. Philip.	Jas. M'Michael, Jr.
1890	James Stalker, D.D.	George E. Philip.	Jas. M'Michael, Jr.
1891	James Stalker, D.D.	George E. Philip.	Jas. M'Michael, Jr.
1892	James Stalker, D.D.	George E. Philip.	Jas. M'Michael, Jr.
1893	James Stalker, D.D.	George E. Philip.	{ Jas. M'Michael, Jr. Matthew Walker.
1894	James Stalker, D.D.	George E. Philip.	Matthew Walker.
1895	James Stalker, D.D.	George E. Philip.	Matthew Walker.
1896	James Stalker, D.D.	George E. Philip.	Matthew Walker.
1897	James Stalker, D.D.	George E. Philip.	Matthew Walker.
1898	James Stalker, D.D.	George E. Philip.	Matthew Walker.

Congregational Treasurer.	Sustentation Treasurer.	Foreign Missions Treasurer.	Year.
William Church.	Neil Caw.	John Williamson.	1872
William Church.	{ Neil Caw. Geo. M. Grierson.	John Williamson.	1873
William Church.	Geo. M. Grierson.	John Williamson.	1874
William Church.	Geo. M. Grierson.	John Williamson.	1875
William Church.	Geo. M. Grierson.	John Williamson.	1876
Geo. M. Grierson.	Geo. M. Grierson.	James White.	1877
Geo. M. Grierson.	Geo. M. Grierson	James White.	1878
Geo. M. Grierson.	Geo. M. Grierson.	James White.	1879
Geo. M. Grierson.	Geo. M. Grierson.	James White.	1880
Geo. M. Grierson.	{ Geo. M. Grierson. Wm. R. Currie.	Don. M'Calman.	1881
Geo. M. Grierson.	Wm. R. Currie.	Peter M'Kichan.	1882
Geo. M. Grierson.	Wm. R. Currie.	Peter M'Kichan.	1883
Robert E. Aitken.	Wm. R. Currie.	Peter M'Kichan.	1884
Robert E. Aitken.	Wm. R. Currie.	Peter M'Kichan.	1885
Robert E. Aitken.	Wm. R. Currie.	George E. Philip.	1886
{ Robert E. Aitken. William Black.	Wm. R. Currie.	{ George E. Philip. Robert Russell.	1887
William Black.	Wm. R. Currie.	Robert Russell.	1888
William Black.	Wm. R. Currie.	Robert Russell.	1889
William Black.	Wm. R. Currie.	Robert Russell.	1890
William Black.	Wm. R. Currie.	Robert Russell.	1891
William Black.	Wm. R. Currie.	Robert Russell.	1892
{ William Black. Jas. M'Michael, Jr.	Wm. R. Currie.	Robert Russell.	1893
Jas. M'Michael, Jr.	Wm. R. Currie.	Robert Russell.	1894
Jas. M'Michael, Jr.	Wm. R. Currie.	Robert Russell.	1895
Jas. M'Michael, Jr.	Wm. R. Currie.	Robert Russell.	1896
Jas. M'Michael, Jr.	Wm. R. Currie.	Robert Russell.	1897
Jas. M'Michael, Jr.	John Stewart.	Robert Russell.	1898

CONVENERS OF STANDING COMMITTEES.

FABRIC.

1844. Allan Buchanan.
1857. Robert Forrester.
1866. John Honeyman.

1868. Thomas Wharrie.
1885. James M'Michael.
1892. Archd. Macfarlane.

1896. Alex. K. Foote.

SEAT-LETTING.

1844. Allan Buchanan.
1846. William Mirrlees.
1849. J. B. Mirrlees.
1851. Allan Buchanan.
1852. William Freebairn.
1871. James C. Wyper.

1872. Geo. M. Grierson.
1877. James F. Barron.
1879. James Imrie.
1891. David MacLean.
1892. Thomas Noble.
1897. William Weatherston.

DAY SCHOOL.

1846. Rev. Samuel Miller.
1849. John Wilson.
1863. William Allan.
1872. James Connell.

1875. David Hay.
1877. R. S. Buchanan.
1877. John M'Kill.
1882. James M'Michael.

1884. *Discontinued.*

POOR FUND.

1848. Peter Lawson.
1853. David C. Nichol.
1863. John Boag.

1868. David Lawson.
1877. Robert Vanhegan.
1882. James M'Michael.

SCHOOLMASTERS' (EDUCATION) FUND.

1849. J. B. Mirrlees.	1875. John Currie.
1851. William Ramsay.	1876. David Greig.
1863. Robert King.	1877. *Discontinued.*

PSALMODY.

1854. William Church.	1881. James Nicholson.
1877. Peter M'Kichan.	1890. William M. Harvey.
1879. James B. Steel.	1895. William Wallace.

1897. John T. Robertson.

DISTRICT MISSION.

1864. Robert Burns.	1882. James B. Steel.
1866. George Young.	1885. { James B. Steel.
1868. William Allan.	{ John Munro.
1872. James Miller.	1887. David Pratt.
1877. Donald M'Calman.	1890. Peter M'Kissock.

1898. Peter Macfarlane.

WELFARE OF YOUTH.

1889. David MacLean.	1890. Peter Macfarlane.

1892. David Rintoul.

STRANGERS.

1890. James Nicholson.	1893. Robert C. Morgan.

EDITORS OF "RECORD" COVER.

1882. Rev. C. A. Salmond, M.A.	1889. Peter Macfarlane.
1887. Rev. J. B. Johnston, B.D.	1893. Robert Craig.

1896. Alexander Ralston.

o

MEMBERSHIP AND CONTRIBUTIONS.

Year.	Membership.	Sustentation Fund.	Foreign Missions.	Ladies' Assoc. for Female Education, etc.	Total Amount Raised.
1844	—	£163	—	—	£764
1845	—	193	£7	—	1426
1846	—	470	30	—	1872
1847	—	709	63	—	2200
1848	750	871	30	—	2238
1849	—	947	127	—	2621
1850	740	985	163	£21	2681
1851	700	1178	152	19	3576
1852	—	1188	117	18	4365
1853	—	1234	143	20	3825
1854	—	1218	185	16	4317
1855	—	1372	179	27	4441
1856	-	1478	165	15	3979
1857	—	1418	150	22	3612
1858	—	1406	162	15	3624
1859	800	1253	167	20	2841
1860	750	1258	168	22	3573
1861	700	1218	181	22	3476
1862	—	1238	186	20	3578
1863	—	1292	188	23	3746
1864	—	1262	188	34	3232
1865	—	1244	190	30	4036
1866	650	1287	193	52	3662
1867	640	1231	180	45	3303
1868	630	1226	184	57	3296
1869	650	1316	176	45	3212
1870	685	1248	175	50	3618
1871	672	1252	168	57	2918
1872	673	1264	174	44	3128
1873	670	1247	178	44	3053
1874	666	1364	172	34	3274
1875	596	1481	150	38	2880
1876	596	1212	150	33	2530
1877	540	787	94	34	2046

Year.	Membership.	Sustentation Fund.	Foreign Missions.	Ladies' Assoc. for Female Education, etc.	Total Amount Raised.
1878	600	£762	£77	£31	£2571
1879	618	744	83	28	2147
1880	648	763	90	27	2125
1881	511	802	112	28	2205
1882	561	836	127	28	3117
1883	662	736	164	30	3146
1884	693	770	180	35	2437
1885	705	708	177	35	2483
1886	682	648	164	29	2419
1887	646	578	142	37	2726
1888	744	582	140	25	2826
1889	878	647	150	23	2983
1890	978	670	164	25	2621
1891	1035	733	174	28	2884
1892	1043	820	181	32	2818
1893	1093	917	215	35	3415
1894	1103	897	251	36	3175
1895	1122	882	260	36	3196
1896	1138	874	262	38	3604
1897	1138	851	242	145	8531
1898	1113	872	282	99	4081
Totals,	—	£54,602	£8572	£1707	£172,453
Average for years tabulated,	765	£993	£159	£35	£3136

Prior to 1868 statistics of *membership* were not called for by the Church. It will, therefore, be noticed that the earlier figures (casually mentioned in congregational records) are evidently stated in round numbers only. Down to 1881, indeed, the roll does not seem to have been purged with the exactitude now considered essential. In that year, however, it was very thoroughly revised, with the result that ninety names were deleted, which accounts for the sudden drop at that time. Since then the figures may be taken as strictly accurate.

MISSIONARY AND CONGREGATIONAL ASSISTANTS.

(1) *In Charge of Anderston District.*

1847. Mr. Allan M'Vean. First Home Missionary of Free St. Matthew's. Went afterwards to Australia.

1850. Mr. William Urie.

1850. Rev. Samuel Kennedy. Ordained minister at Stewarton in 1852.

1852. Rev. George Wisely. Afterwards missionary in the Wynds, and assistant at Leghorn. Ordained minister at Malta in 1854, and received the degree of D.D. from Aberdeen University in 1894.

1853. Rev. Peter C. Purves. Ordained minister at Morebattle in 1855. Now minister at Granton.

1853. Rev. Joseph Davidson. Ordained minister at Saltcoats in 1855, and afterwards translated to Rothesay. Married Dr. Miller's sister-in-law.

1855. Mr. Christison. Removed to Edinburgh.

1862. Mr. Alexander Stirling. Ordained minister at Monkton in 1865. Now minister at York.

1865. Mr. John Bethune. Ordained minister at Portmoak in 1880.

1867. Mr. Alexander Linn. Ordained minister of St. Fergus in 1871. Translated to Cranstonhill in 1877.

1867. Mr. David S. Dykes. At first assistant to Mr. Linn; latterly in full charge. Ordained minister at Gamrie in 1872.

1869. Mr. Thomas Stewart.

1872. Mr. David S. Hamilton. Ordained minister at Symington, Ayrshire, in 1874.

1874. Rev. Donald Meiklejohn. Last missionary at Anderston.

Many of the above (especially Rev. Messrs. Kennedy, Wisely, Purves, and Davidson), though responsible in the first instance for the Mission at Anderston, gave large help also in the work of the congregation.

(2) *In Charge of Springbank District.*

1881. Rev. Frank S. Gardiner, M.A. Ordained minister at Coleraine in 1882. Now minister of Kingstown.

1882. Rev. David Ross, M.A. Ordained minister at Crathie in 1883. Afterwards translated to Perth, Western Australia.

1883. Rev. H. Y. Reyburn, B.D. Ordained minister at Leven in 1884. Afterwards translated to Kirkintilloch.

1884. Mr. William Ewing, student. Ordained in St. Matthew's as missionary at Tiberias in 1888. Now minister in Birmingham.

1885. Mr. Robert H. Logan, M.A., student. Ordained minister at Dundee in 1889.

1885. Mr. James Allan, lay missionary. Accepted similar appointment in Moray Church, Edinburgh.

1886. Rev. J. B. Johnstone, B.D. Ordained minister at Falkirk in 1888. Married a daughter of Mr. Jas. M'Michael, elder. Author of *Place-Names of Scotland.*

1888. Rev. Robert M. Gray, M.A. Ordained in St. Matthew's as minister at Bombay in 1890.

1890. Rev. William Hay, B.D. Ordained minister at Ayr in 1892.

1892. Rev. Robert Scrymgeour, M.A. Ordained minister at Monikie in 1894. Translated to Jersey in 1898.

1894. Rev. Robert G. Philip, M.A. Ordained minister at Glencairn in 1896.

1896. Rev. David Young, M.A. Ordained minister at Partick in 1898.

1898. Rev. R. D. Robertson. Present missionary assistant.

Nearly all of the above, though responsible in the first instance for the Mission at Springbank, gave large help also in the work of the congregation.

(3) *Occasional and Temporary.*

1862. Rev. George Proudfoot. Appointed chaplain to City Poor House about 1863.

1863. Rev. Robert Mackellar. Ordained minister at Gourock in 1864.

1868. Rev. John R. Elder, M.A. Ordained minister of Cromarty in 1869. Afterwards translated to Arrochar. Married a daughter of Mr. John Wilson, elder.

1873. Rev. J. P. Lilley, M.A. Ordained minister at Arbroath in 1874.

1874. Rev. George Morice (late of New Zealand).

1875. Rev. J. C. Connell. Ordained minister at Thurso in 1876.

1876. Rev. A. Wright, M.A. Ordained minister at Musselburgh in 1876.

1876. Rev. P. Barclay, M.A. Retired minister of Napier, New Zealand.

1880. Rev. H. H. Currie, B.D. Ordained minister at Keig in 1880.

1880. Rev. David Miller, M.A. Ordained minister at Stranraer in 1881.

1892. Mr. John Tudhope, student. Ordained minister of Queen's Road Church, Liverpool, in 1895.

1893. Mr. J. H. Maclean, student. Ordained missionary at Madras in 1896.

1894. Rev. Hugh MacLuskie. Ordained minister at Irvine in 1895.

1895. Rev. C. W. Fleming, B.D. Appointed to Indive, South Africa, in 1898.

1896. Rev. A. R. Gordon, M.A.⎱ Ordained minister at Monikie
1897. Rev. A. R. Gordon, M.A.⎰   in 1898.

1898. Rev. John Fulton, B.D. Son of Mr. John Fulton, elder. Present winter assistant.

Down to 1880 these appointments were usually made for several months at a time, and had specially in view the supply of St. Matthew's pulpit during the absence of Dr. Miller through illness. From 1892 they were made for five or six months in winter only, and had specially in view the charge of Bible class and assistance in visitation.